SIMON VARWELL

Simon Varwell is a compulsive traveller, a keen amateur photographer, and spends too much time having 'what if . . .' moments. 'Up the Creek Without a Mullet' tells the story of one such moment, and is his first book.

Simon was born in 1978 and grew up in Benbecula in the Western Isles. He is married and lives in Inverness.

His website can be found at:

www.simonvarwell.co.uk

Dear Susan,

Thanks for agreeing with me on the Pyramids!

Best wishes,

[signature]

UP THE CREEK WITHOUT A MULLET

A hair-brained journey across the globe

Simon Varwell

SANDSTONEPRESS
HIGHLAND | SCOTLAND

First published in Great Britain 2010
Sandstone Press Ltd
PO Box 5725
One High Street
Dingwall
Ross-shire
IV15 9WJ
Scotland

www.sandstonepress.com

Editor: Robert Davidson

The publisher acknowledges subsidy from the Scottish Arts Council
towards publication of this volume.

ISBN-10: 1-905207-34-4
ISBN-13: 978-1-905207-34-3

Cover design by Raspberryhmac, Edinburgh

Typeset in Linotype Sabon by Iolaire Typesetting, Newtonmore
Printed and bound by Atheneum Press, Gateshead

For Nicole

Contents

Contents

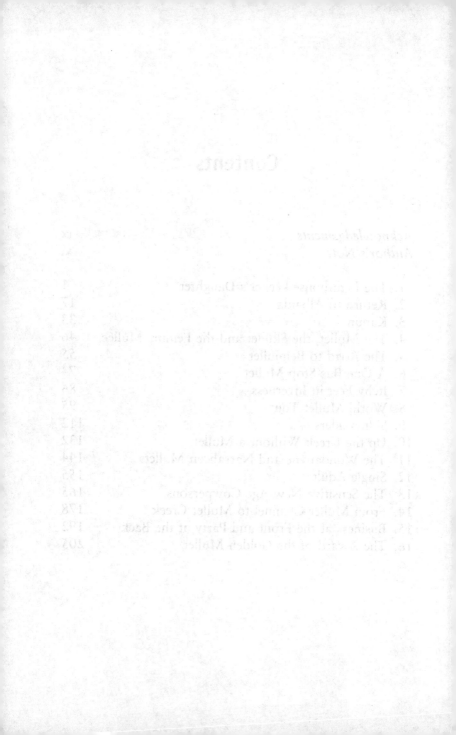

Acknowledgements

To everyone mentioned in this book, you've helped make the story what it is and deserve a thank you. Thank you.

To everyone not mentioned in this book but who nevertheless feel they deserve a thank you too, you're probably right. Thank you.

Author's Note

10% of the author's royalties are going to aidconvoy.net, the humanitarian organisation mentioned in the story. Your support for this good cause in buying this book is very much appreciated.

The author is grateful to Donald S Murray for his kind permission to reprint the poem 'The Lighthouse-keeper's Daughter', taken from his collection 'West-coasters' by Cuan Ard Press.

Author's Note

ONE

The Lighthouse-keeper's Daughter

Eyes wide open, but not staring too obviously. Head turns from side to side but not too conspicuously. Don't want to attract attention, not in a place like this. Breathe normally, keep watching, keep walking, keep waiting.

Noise. Dust. Traffic. Heat.

In the middle of it all, though, a sighting.

'There, three o'clock!' The intensity of the whisper betrays the excitement of the catch.

'Ah yes, good one. And over there, another, in the café, nice long one.'

A pause.

'By that doorway . . . man, check that out.'

'He's confident. He knows he's got it and he wants the world to see.'

'More . . . there's two of them, together! This is crazy!'

'. . . and a female one . . . and another! Incredible!'

'If things carry on like this, it's going to beat Prague!'

They did; and it did.

We were in the mountainous, dusty north of Albania in the autumn of 2001, in the run-down, yet likeably chaotic town of Shkodra. For several weeks, my friend Niall and I had been travelling through central Europe and on to the Balkans, backpacking our way from Frankfurt to Cairo, celebrating the end of university, and postponing the inevitable search for work that was waiting for us back home in Scotland.

Over our four month trip we took in fifteen countries, with

major highlights including the magnificent scenery, language and beer of Croatia, learning about the emerging democracies of post-communist Europe, and the changing shape of the Middle East as the Twin Towers fell.

Both being football fans, Niall and I went to as many local matches as we could, including a Slovenian third division tie, a dreary goalless draw played in the town of Piran, but held in a splendid setting overlooked by a ruined castle. Another game was a Slovakian first division match in Trencin, a pretty town in the west of the country whose skyline was dominated by two things: a beautiful hilltop castle, and the massive flood-lights of the football stadium, four unnecessarily enormous grey lollipops that could be seen from miles around. We were told by a local that when they were installed the first switch-on overwhelmed the local power supply and plunged half of Trencin into darkness. There was even a Scottish connection at one of our matches, when our visit to Budapest coincided with a heated Hungary v Romania 2002 World Cup qualifier, which we were surprised and delighted to discover was refereed by top Scottish official Hugh Dallas.

Due to lucky coincidences, we even appeared in a Bulgarian magazine and on Israeli television when features were done by local journalists about the hostels in Sofia and Tel Aviv we were staying in. Elsewhere, the expedition saw us travel on far too many cramped buses and meet more Australians than I thought existed.

I also discovered rather a lot about mullets.

Niall had been a keen mullet-spotter for years and, as our unofficial trip diarist and archivist, kept a keen record of those ubiquitous 1980s haircuts that we encountered through our trip.

Those weren't the only statistics he kept, though. To pass the time we formulated a lot of 'top fives' on our trip. From the 'top five buildings we've seen', to the 'top five places', and from the sublime 'top five awful accommodation', to the ridiculous (and this was my personal favourite) 'top five people we've met who we'd have got on better with, were it not for the language barrier'.

We even spent a very bored evening in a quiet youth hostel in the historic Arab quarter of the Israeli town of Akko, watching the Jordanian version of 'Who Wants to be a Millionaire', and ranking all the people we'd met on our travels up to that point on four personality criteria and imagining which of them would get on best with each other should they ever meet.

Looking back, I think this stands as a warning about what happens when you spend up to four months, more or less twenty four hours a day, in the same company.

The mullet league table, however, was the major endeavour.

Top of his – our – league so far had been Prague, one of the first cities we went to. It boasted a healthy dose of denim-jacket wearing, rock-star mops, short at the front and long at the back, looks that were prevalent in post-Communist Europe.

As we continued on our travels, I became bemused, intrigued and then eventually engrossed in this comparative study. Any walk we took became a mullet safari. Any trip out to a shop, museum or pub became a chance to give a town a rating against which it could be compared to other places – at least in the minds of two bored Scottish backpackers.

As I say, though, Prague eventually met its match in Shkodra, in the fading summer of the Albanian mountains. As we gingerly explored this decrepit but bustling conurbation, we paid little attention to our Communist-era hotel with its total lack of running water or electricity and hazy views across the smog-filled concrete expanse of the town centre.

We were only briefly distracted by the town's mosque which we were told was originally three storeys high but was now only two, because it had sunk into the soft ground on which it was built.

The main attraction for us was not even the nearby Rozafa Castle, built above the town and offering stunning views of the dark mountains and countryside incised by three vast rivers. Not even the fact that, according to legend, the castle had mysteriously collapsed a number of times during construction, and was only able to be completed after a young mother was imprisoned in a tower as a sacrifice, and whose baby was still able to be fed thanks to two strategically placed holes in the wall. According to our tour guide, mothers still smeared condensation from the ruined walls on to their breasts, to encourage lactation.

Yes, Shkodra was that kind of town.

Neither did we pay much heed to the urgent warnings we received from locals as soon as we'd got out of the taxi we'd taken from the border with Montenegro, about three Czech backpackers who had completely vanished in the town some weeks before. Or to the armed, balaclava-clad men who mingled with the furious traffic on the edge of town as night fell, whom we observed from what we hoped was a safe distance (but who we later discovered were simply traffic policemen, disguising their identity in a country where the mafia was rife and policing a dangerous vocation).

No, instead, our abiding memory of Shkodra was the utter, phenomenal, unbridled abundance of mullets. We are not talking a healthy showing of an occasional mullet – we are talking about a torrent. It was like a uniform, with singles, couples and groups of mullets wandering the pot-holed streets of this strange town, usually wearing Eastern Europe's fashion standard, the blue shell-suit, as if the last couple of decades had passed the town by.

The sheer, overwhelming consistency of mulletry in the town, including some incredible femme mullées (female mullets) confirmed to us that this was truly Mullet City, the capital of mullets, and by far the run-away leader of the mullet league table.

Although our travels from then on continued to be a grand adventure, nowhere came close to Shkodra for mulletry, and nowhere contributed so much to my appreciation and understanding of the haircut. From that point on, I was hooked. I was a real mullet-spotter.

A mulletophile.

Let me take you a year further on in time, to the summer of 2002, to my newly adopted city of Inverness, and to a job setting up the students' association of the embryonic University of the Highlands and Islands. Smaller than Aberdeen, where I had spent the previous five years studying and working, the Capital of the Highlands, as Inverness calls itself, is a beautiful city – well-kept, compact, thriving, prosperous and very touristy. It is the main base for exploration of Loch Ness and its monsterish resident, the beautiful isle of Skye, and more beaches, bagpipes, castles, mountains and distilleries than you could shake a 'See you, Jimmy' hat at.

Although Aberdeen had an impressive mulletry, crowned one beautiful day by the sight of a purple punk femme mullée, Inverness had the bonus that its modest collection of mullets could be seen on a regular basis. There was the mullet bin man. The mullet white van man frequently seen driving around town. The skullet (receding mullet) who was waiting outside the Clydesdale Bank on Academy Street every Tuesday morning. And the man I saw in lots of pubs who looked like he'd just walked out of a second-rate German rock band.

I was mullet-hunting on my own, however: I was over a hundred miles away from Niall, with whom I had spent every day for four months during our travels. He was back in Aberdeen, working as a kitchen porter, a job that somehow managed to finance a copious amount of drinking and partying. He was also living in a remote castle on the Aberdeenshire coast.

Well, not quite a castle. It was actually an old house built on the site of a castle, from which one solitary and disconcertingly top-heavy wall was just about standing despite the ravages of the North Sea winds. It was half an hour's drive north of Aberdeen, off the main road, along a long farm track, and out to the edge of a peninsula which boasted two deserted beaches, plenty fresh sea air, and only puffins and other seabirds for neighbours.

Niall had moved in there with a group of friends who were all looking for somewhere off the beaten track that could contain their voracious appetite for humungous parties, at which DJ friends of theirs would play through the small hours and on until the sun broke out from the sea and bathed the castle and its wasted party-goers in fiery red sunshine.

I went there several times throughout the year of Niall's residency. I enjoyed scouring the beaches, sitting in the garden watching the sea, capturing the stunning sunrises on my camera, exploring the numerous nooks, crannies and hidden rooms the old house boasted, and experiencing the all-night parties at which I would meet some fascinating characters, one or two of whom even occasionally retained the power of speech.

One particular party, I recall, took place in the middle of the summer, a time of year when the north of Scotland had barely a few hours of darkness, and the sun would rise long before most sensible people. Unless of course they'd been up all night. On this occasion I'd taken a break at about 4am to go outside, chill out and watch the sun, a fierce orange disc, heave slowly out of the North Sea. A couple of hours later I headed inside again only to be complimented on the healthy tan I'd just acquired.

It was a magnetic place. So much so that a little idea came into my mind, and when I explained it to Niall on the phone, he was in agreement. Our thinking was this: Inverness gets lots of tourists. Lots and lots. In the peak season you can't move in the city centre for folk taking photos of themselves, each other, the river and the castle, and generally getting in the way of locals like myself who were simply trying to go about their daily lives without having to stop every minute to step around an excited gang of Italians or Americans. Aberdeen, however, gets none. Despite being in some lovely countryside with lots to see and do, its reputation as a rather dour, grey city at the heart of Europe's oil industry deters many visitors who instead just plump for Inverness and the Highlands.

Having been tourists across Europe for many weeks, Niall and I were interested in looking at Scotland with fresh eyes. What if those visitors could be tempted by something different? Like free accommodation in a wild old castle on the coast?

So it was that, over the course of the first tourist season I lived in Inverness, I would tell any backpackers or tourists I got chatting to in my local pub – the Harlequin – about my friend in Aberdeen who lived in a castle and had free accommodation, should they make the two and a half hour journey east. Most thought I was a bit of a lunatic. Some were curious for long enough to speak to Niall on the phone to confirm this was not a wind up. A Canadian, a Dane and two Belgians even trusted us enough to do the journey and had a great time there with Niall.

Apart from making a negligible contribution to the tourist economy of rural Aberdeenshire, it didn't really achieve much. It was made a few evenings in the pub slightly more entertaining and off-beat, but didn't leave me with any sense of achievement.

In any case, the idea died off with the end of the tourist season and the news from Niall that he was going to move to South Korea to teach English, after a ghostly voice in the castle allegedly told him to do just that.

I'd heard of poltergeists haunting old castles, but careers guidance ghosts? That was a new one on me.

It must have been a good party that particular night.

So for me, life went back to normal. I ambled along, working away at my job, enjoying the travels it involved around the Highlands and islands and further afield, making new friends, and settling comfortably into Inverness.

Life was good. It was busy, sociable and stimulating, but predictable.

Until, one quiet day, in late 2002 while bored at work, when it changed forever.

Have you ever wondered how the world of work coped before the internet? And I don't just mean the internet in terms of a place for organisations to communicate and advertise. I mean those occasional – alright, frequent – moments when you find yourself with nothing to do, or no motivation, and you resort to reading the news, checking your email, or visiting friends' websites.

I'd been having lots of those moments of late. Occasionally, I would browse websites to further my interest in Albania. My first visit was in 1999, with Kieran, a friend who I knew from Aberdeen but who now lived in Brighton and ran a small international aid charity that had worked in various parts of Eastern Europe.

That summer, there was a war in Kosovo, a province of Serbia which had a majority Albanian population and which bordered Albania itself. It was the final stage in the collapse of Yugoslavia. War and ethnic cleansing was followed, painfully late, by international intervention that brought some semblance of peace and stability. My university's students' association, in which Kieran and I were involved, organised a lorry-load of aid as part of a convoy from across Britain. He and I, along with many others, headed across Europe to meet with student leaders in Kosovo, give what help we could, and learn something about the terrible destruction of what we found to be a beautiful and hospitable country.

The journey itself was an adventure – ten countries in all, the latter stages of which saw us sail from the south of Italy to Greece, and then drive north to Kosovo through Macedonia. However, we were held up at the Greek-Macedonian border for some considerable time, the Macedonian officials seemingly suspicious of our motives. In the complicated political dynamics of south-eastern Europe at the time, the Macedonians, a Slavic nation like the Serbs, appeared reluctant to give too much free passage to aid groups like ours who were perceived (wrongly) as wanting only to help the Albanians and not also Kosovo's Serbian minority. Furthermore, Macedonia feared a similar conflict being sparked off with its own large Albanian minority.

A Swiss-based Albanian trucker we befriended at the border, who was heading to Kosovo too, was given a much harder time than we were at the hands of the border guards, and was in the end let through only after a large sum of money had changed hands.

Eventually, after about twenty-four hours of deadlock, including expensive phonecalls home to media and political contacts, we were granted passage by the Macedonians at the dead of night, but only under a police escort who took us non-stop across the country to the border with Kosovo. To this day we still don't know the full story of the strings that were pulled in our favour, but we understand that very senior politicians in the British Foreign Office were involved somewhere along the line.

On our way home from Kosovo, we took a different route, bypassing Macedonia in favour of Albania. This was partly due to our experiences on the outbound journey, but also because of a huge Albanian flag which some Kosovan kids had painted on the side of our lorry. At the time it seemed like an innocent idea, but later on, as we prepared to leave, some friendly Kosovan Albanians warned us that it would not be the best PR message to have the flag on show if returning via the highways and byways of Macedonia.

Such is the nature of the politics of identity in the region that it was probably very wise counsel. The displaying of Albanian flags in non-Albanian areas, or indeed certain other flags in Albanian areas, could be ignorant or dangerous actions. For instance, we heard a story about one of the very first aid workers to arrive in Kosovo after the war, who spoke to some ethnic Albanian locals in Serbian, and was killed for his trouble.

Even the name 'Kosovo' is a political hot potato. 'Kosovo' is the official and internationally-recognised name for the province, but that derives from the Serbian name and spelling. Albanians spell and pronounce it 'Kosova'.

On our alternative route, we found Albania itself to be, thanks to forty years of economic stagnation under Communism, almost in a worse condition than Kosovo. The crumbling, pot-holed roads, little better than tracks in places, inflicted a heavy toll on Kieran's lorry. We broke down in Albania's northern Highlands, the roughest corner of Europe's roughest country, and since then I've been fascinated by the rugged beauty of the place.

When Niall and I returned a couple of years later on our big travels, my love for it only strengthened. The dramatic scenery, the friendly people, the mysterious and turbulent history, the chaos, the energy, and of course the mullets . . . it all made me think seriously about finding a way back.

I was still in regular email contact with Niall, who kept me up to date with his news as he settled into teaching English in Daegu, a large and busy South Korean city. What I enjoyed most of all was being able to tell him about the mullets I saw in Inverness and on my travels for work. All sorts of mullets – subtle ones on businessmen in suits, flamboyant mullets worn with pride by alternative-looking types, or just the regular kind you'd see on someone straight out of an American trailer park. South Korea wasn't good hunting grounds for mullets, and so I think Niall appreciated my updates.

Sadly, however, I found that others did not share my understanding or appreciation for the world's most curious follicular manifestation. Usually when starting to talk about mullets to my friends, or to tourists I met in the Harlequin pub, which was near my flat and which sat conveniently next to two youth hostels and overlooked the castle and the river, I would be viewed with either alarm or suspicion. Folk would turn away and lose interest, friends would tell me to change the subject, and worried German backpackers would put an arm round each other and leave quickly.

Niall would have understood. He'd have wanted to while away the long evenings with deep discussions about mullets. But he was on the other side of the world.

If I was honest, I was a little envious. Life in Inverness was great, but the idea of throwing caution to the wind and launching myself into a new and unfamiliar culture to teach a language I'd spoken with, I must confess, some reasonable competence for around a quarter of a century sounded like an exciting challenge.

I'd love to teach English in somewhere like Albania, I thought. Still a part of Europe, but different enough to be a real challenge, an eye-opener. I spent more and more time both at home and in work looking at websites about Albania – cultural, tourist and political websites – just anything that told me a little more about the land, the language, the places and the people.

That afternoon, when everything changed, where the roots of this story lie, was an inauspicious one. A busy day, lots of paperwork to get through and emails to reply to. But rather than dealing with that, I found myself browsing some Albanian tourist information websites, which were both worrying in how out of date they were and wryly amusing in how bad the translation into English was.

But my heart missed a beat and I sat bolt upright when, on a page about the history of Albania, I found the following . . .

Tirana was founded in 1614 by Sulejman Pasha from the village of Mullet. In the beginning, he built a mosque, a bakery and a Turkish sauna. Two centuries later the city was led by the Toptani family from Kruja.

I read it again. '. . . from the village of Mullet.'
A village.
In Albania.
Called Mullet.
Mullet.
Oh boy. This was incredible.

I read it again: In *the beginning, he built a mosque, a bakery and a Turkish sauna.*

Well, old Sulejman really got his priorities right – prayers, pies and perspiration. What more could you want from a capital city?

Two centuries later the city was led by the Toptani family from Kruja.

Wow. Those pies must have been good to have convinced the Toptanis to move in.

I searched a bit more. Besides having Sulejman as a famous son, Mullet also apparently came to prominence during the 1999 war in Kosovo, when tens of thousands of refugees fled over the border into Albania, and were housed in refugee camps. I came across references to one of these camps on a charity's website – the Mullet Camp.

The Mullet Camp? How amazing would this have been if it had not been a refugee camp in Mullet, but an actual Mullet Camp? Imagine the scene – dozens, if not hundreds of young Albanian children, away from their parents for a week or two of the summer holidays, bussed into the camp where they would be given a mullet haircut by a mulletrician (well, what else would you call a hairdresser who gives you a mullet?), and taught all sorts of lessons about how to nurture and respect their mullets, and about how to maintain the mullet as the greatest haircut in Albania.

I am not sure if that thought was scary or wonderful. But perhaps thankfully it was just my imagination. I hoped.

But still . . . what an amazing discovery. A village called Mullet.

I had an idea forming.

'You're going to do what??' exclaimed Niall on the telephone one evening.

'Go to Mullet, and see if it has a mullet there.'

'Why?'

'Well. . .' I stared out of my living room window but found no inspiration in the darkness and unrelenting rain. I had to improvise as I hadn't really thought about these sorts of complicated questions yet. 'Because if it is called Mullet, there has to be one there. After all, it is Albania. But wait, there's more!'

And there was. My discovery of Mullet, Albania, had made me wonder if there were others out there. By the end of that afternoon, in which all thoughts of work were thrown aside, I had discovered two other amazing place names, and I told Niall all about them.

Mullet Creek, in that centre of Australian mulletry, Queensland.

Mullet Bay, a beautiful resort on the Caribbean island of St Martins.

'. . . and I'm going to visit them all, and find mullets there!' I exclaimed triumphantly, with the determination of an emperor declaring war on his neighbours.

'Those others aren't even proper Mullet towns – they're a bay and a creek, and so they're probably named after the fish not the haircut!!'

'They still count! A mullet is a mullet.'

Niall must have wondered what he had created. His fanaticism had been overtaken by my objective to visit the mullets of the world. I was enthused – he was probably just scared. But I had it all thought through. I was going ahead with it. And I was going to find Mullets. Mullets in Mullets, even.

Over the next few weeks, my enthusiasm for this new idea did not wane. I was glad – it was too good a project to get bored with, and the more I thought of it, the more fantastic it sounded.

To visit these diverse parts of the world would be fun in itself, but to go mullet-spotting there would allow a totally unique form of comparative study of these towns that had nothing in common except their names.

I was a bit worried about one rather small detail – money. Sadly, I had a full-time job, a mortgage, and a savings account balance that at the last count stood at four pence. It would not be easy.

That didn't put me off, though – I could visit one a year, I figured, saving hard for the holiday and savouring each experience over twelve long months until the next one came round. It was just a shame the Mullets were all such a long way away, and would require a lot of time and expense.

However, not long after, something quite unexpected dropped on to my mat early one morning in the post.

The Lighthouse-keeper's Daughter
(for Mairead)

When she was younger,
she used to dream
of how the lighthouse-beam might bring
visitors to their gate.

Castaways on the peninsula.
Friends from the fishing-port
whose fathers hers
held in safety with his light.
Now she is circled by a city's brightness,
ushering people to a room
where projectors beam
stories on a screen.

A long way from Belmullet to Dundee,
headland to a heartland,
and there must be days,
she longs for the predictable

Solitary gleam that guided
her and others,
the reassurance of a silence
punctuated by tide and light.

Donald S Murray

Belmullet. Belmullet. It just sounds right. Sure, Mullet Bay is great, but it is two words. Belmullet is just one. Short, snappy, and with 'mullet' as the object rather than the adjective. Of course, nothing beats the purity and unadulteratedness of Mullet itself, in Albania.

But still. Belmullet. Almost French . . . beautiful mullet. Belmullet. You had to like it.

The poem was written by a former English teacher of mine back in Benbecula, an island in the Western Isles on which I had grown up, but which I had left to go to university. He also wrote short stories and poems, and had a number of publications to his name. When my brother had gone back to Benbecula on a brief holiday he had picked up a copy of Donald S Murray's latest book for me.

It was a collection of poems about the west coasts of Ireland and Scotland. *The Lighthouse-keeper's Daughter* was typical of them – they mostly explored themes relating to how those who left such parts of the world would come to miss them and regret the move away – just like he supposed Mairead in this poem might do. Frankly, I wouldn't have blamed her either, living in Dundee.

But where in Ireland was Belmullet? What was so captivating about the lighthouse-beam? Would the town be a haven of mullets? Maybe it was the lighthouse-beam that attracted them, a kind of pied piper of mullets. But in any case, it was another Mullet, worth visiting, worth investigating, and perhaps a close one. Would it be easy to visit? Would anyone still be living there, or were they all working in Dundee cinemas? And who the hell was Mairead?

Meanwhile, things were progressing sooner than I thought with the other Mullets. The big one, in particular. *La piece de la resistance*. Mullet itself.

Kieran, with whom I went on the aid convoy to Kosovo in 1999, had been spending the last few years building and developing his own charitable organisation, and he had done quite a bit of work in Kosovo, Albania and Ukraine since our trip together.

I had really appreciated that experience with him in Kosovo, seeing some of the terrible effects of war and the terrible driving of the Kosovans. Things took a turn for the dramatic when we broke down in Albania on our way home of course, but we made it back, with frayed nerves but at least still in one piece.

I had always hoped to make it out with him on another convoy, but I was in the north of Scotland, and he was in the south of England. Whenever I had the time to come, I had no money to get down. When I had cash, there was always something else getting in the way. Like his ageing truck breaking down again and having a holiday at the garage. Perhaps it was not to be.

That was until the summer of 2003, when he announced his plans to take a break from recent work in Ukraine to rediscover contacts in Albania, see how the country was developing, and if feasible recommence runs of humanitarian and development aid to Albania. He invited me along.

Oh boy, this was just too good a chance to miss out on. Albania was not a massive country. Mullet was not far from the capital. I could do it. I wanted to do it. I had to do it.

My first Mullet!

TWO

Return to Albania

I think my abiding memory of Kieran will be of that time when we broke down on our way home from Kosovo. It was 1999, a scorching hot August day in the Albanian mountains, and the truck, an old Dodge 50 van formerly used by British Gas inspectors, still with telephone numbers from the 1980s on the underside of the driver's sun shield, had ground to a clunking halt.

Cars and other technical things are not my strong point (I can't even wire a plug), but the driveshaft, which I was led to believe is quite important to proceedings, had simply given up the ghost and clunked on to the dusty track that formed the main highway through the mountains from the Kosovan border to the more populated south of the country.

Despite the heat, the stress, the oil, and the fact that neither of us knew what on earth we were going to do on this wild mountainside with an ageing vehicle that had died an abrupt death, Kieran was dressed as immaculately as ever – sturdy boots, neat dark trousers, white shirt, and velvet waistcoat. Not that I want to paint a picture of him as a pretentious sharp-suiter, or even as a hobbit impersonator, which he was frequently taken for with his waistcoats and curly hair. Rather, he was more like the gentleman abroad, perhaps a Michael Palin, taking everything in his stride, and keeping a gentle tone and warm smile at all times.

So it was, four years later, in July 2003, that that we headed off back to the land of the mountains. Kieran, having focused on his projects in Ukraine in recent months, was inspired to rediscover Albanian opportunities for his organisation after gaining the acquaintance of a professional clown, Peat. Devil-stick Peat, to use his stage name, was a juggler, children's entertainer, and general fool at touristy castles in the English countryside, at historical festivals and wherever else there was a need for long hair, silly jokes and uncannily good circus skills.

Kieran had met him through a mutual contact. Peat had also been in Albania a couple of years before and he too was keen to revisit the country. He had worked for a UNICEF-sponsored programme educating children about the dangers of weapons, landmines and the Mafia, and there were a few people he was interested in looking up.

I was, I told Kieran, really looking forward to coming along, because it would allow me to contribute something more to his organisation. I'd heard all about his last four years' work, but had not directly contributed since first working with him in 1999. It would also be a chance to see a beautiful country again, and a constructive use of my two weeks' leave in the summer.

What I didn't tell him was that the main reason I was coming along was to see if we could do a quick detour to a village called Mullet. There was plenty time to let him into the slightly less cerebral side to my motivation later on, I figured.

We would travel in the battle-hardened (and several-times repaired) truck that had survived Albania four years previously, and our route was to be England to Belgium, then a quick drive through a handful of central European countries, and along the northern Adriatic coast until we reached Albania. First, I had to fly down from Inverness to Gatwick airport, just south of London, where Kieran and Peat would meet me.

That was a journey in itself. Not because it is a long or arduous flight (it's barely an hour and a half), but because the difference in climate between London and the Highlands is at its greatest in the summer. Inverness, surrounded by beautiful mountains and bathing in fresh, unpolluted air that comes through the Moray Firth from the North Sea, is lucky to see temperatures of much over twenty degrees. London, however, with its smog, pollution and hot, sticky summers, often feels like a different country (though of course the nationalist in me tells myself that, actually, it is). Good job I lived in the Highlands, really – for me, the likes of the south coast of England counted as the tropics.

I landed at Gatwick after an uneventful flight, picked up my bag at the reclaim, and went outside the terminal. I switched on my mobile.

It rang straight away, and a slow, West Country accent spoke to me when I answered.

'Hello, it's Peat.' It was, it seemed, Peat. 'How's it going?'

'Not bad thanks! This is Simon,' I said, somewhat redundantly.

'Where are you?'

'Outside the entrance. Or the exit. It might be both.'

'Which entrance, mate?'

This stumped me. Of course, Gatwick was an airport that probably had more exits than Inverness airport had scheduled daily flights. Including the early morning newspaper and mail run to Stornoway on the isle of Lewis. That's a fun one to take, incidentally, if you don't fancy the regular passenger flight – most seats are taken up by bundled up boxes and papers, and there are only around two or three seats available at the back for passengers. When I took it on a work trip once, I and my sole fellow traveller could see right the way up the aisle into the open cockpit, and I almost expected to see live chickens or goats roaming the cabin.

'Erm . . . I'm not sure,' I replied to Peat, 'I just followed signs for exits.' I looked around for something that was distinctive. 'There's lots of people. And a road. And some buildings opposite.' I wasn't being much help. I described what I was wearing, so he would recognise me.

'Right, I've got long hair and a beard,' said Peat, with not a hint of impatience. 'Stay there, I'll find you.'

A couple of minutes later Peat called back.

'I think I can see you. What are you standing next to?'

'A row of pillars,' I said, looking around me, 'and an empty newspaper stand.'

Suddenly, there was a tap on my shoulder, and I turned round to face what appeared to be Jesus in a UNICEF t-shirt.

'I'm Peat,' said Peat, closing his phone and extending a hand.

'I'm Simon,' I said. 'Nice to meet you. Where's Kieran?'

'On a verge by one of the airport car parks. He's waiting with the truck – it's broken down.'

I allowed myself a wry smile.

'I have a bad feeling about this,' I said.

This was going to be an interesting trip.

'I'm from Glastonbury', explained Peat, 'which most people don't think exists except for four days when the music festival comes to town.'

We were sitting in the sunshine on a grass verge just a short walk from the terminal, me on my rucksack and Peat on what appeared to be a large picnic hamper. Kieran was gazing under the bonnet of the truck and talking on his mobile to a mechanic friend.

'But that's not to say there's similarities,' Peat went on. 'There's still a big hippy and alternative population in the village of Glastonbury, and it's always been very independent-minded. A couple of years back, McDonald's opened up a restaurant there. It only lasted a short while before it was burned down. It took the police until two weeks afterwards to establish it was arson. Ironic, really.'

'Why?' I asked.

'Because everyone else in the village knew it was arson two weeks *beforehand*.'

I laughed. The mention of McDonald's reminded me of the fact that due to my rush to leave the flat that morning and my flight being low-cost and food-free, I'd not eaten anything all day. As if by a feat of corporate magic, I noticed a McDonald's just along the road from us.

'I'm hungry,' I said.

'There! What did I tell you?' exclaimed Kieran cheerily, as he hung up the phone and came to join us. 'What did I say on our way to the airport, Peat?'

'That Simon always needs food,' Peat replied in his Somerset drawl, turning to me with a grin. 'And if we want to stop you being in a bad mood on the trip we've got to keep you stocked up!'

This was true. The fact I was relatively slim in build didn't stop me having a huge appetite, and especially when I was on the move, my needs in life were simple – plenty sleep and plenty food. I was twenty-five, and could still get away with eating more or less what I wanted on only the barest minimum of exercise.

'Well, I'm off to McDonald's,' I said. 'Anyone want anything?'

'No thanks,' said Peat, unsurprisingly. 'But if I had some quick-drying cement I'd come with you to visit the bathroom!'

I returned some minutes later, Big Mac in hand, to find that Kieran's mechanic friend was on his way with a tow-truck, and it looked very much like we weren't going anywhere, certainly not in the Dodge. All we could do was sit back, relax and enjoy the sunshine.

Peat opened his picnic hamper, which was actually his box of entertainers' tricks, fished out four plastic clubs, and began juggling. After a few minutes, he got bored of that, and took out three sticks. These were, he explained, the devilsticks from which he took his stage name. Holding one stick in each hand, the aim was to keep the third stick in the air by hitting it backwards and forwards between your hands.

'Most of my tricks are self-taught,' Peat said as he performed, his actions so nonchalant, so well practised they seemed second nature. 'I lived in Wales for four months some years back, in a run-down house in the middle of nowhere, and just practised and practised. Barely saw anyone the whole time, just juggled and did devilsticks.'

He twirled the third stick round one of the sticks in his hands, threw it high up in the air, caught it again, and tapped it side to side like a pendulum with the two others.

Then he put the sticks away and picked up a small velvet bag, which he held in front of his mouth. His face looked strained, as if he was going to be sick . . . and all of a sudden out popped a ping-pong ball into the bag. Peat put on a mock-surprised look, one no doubt perfected through many performances, and put a long finger into his mouth, searching for any other obstructions. Another ping-pong ball came out, and no sooner had he put this into the bag than another began slowly forcing its way out of his mouth. Then another one came, and another, and after about twenty small white balls had slid, bounced and jumped out of his mouth into the bag, Kieran and I were still no wiser as to how he managed the trick.

Not every aid convoy had its own resident Fool, so in this sense we were privileged. This was only the start of Peat's box of magic tricks, too.

I'll not bore you with the mechanics of it all (largely because I didn't understand myself), but it turned out the elderly truck had well and truly died. Kieran was able to get a tow from his mechanic friend back to his flat in Brighton, where we resorted to Plan B, the charity's other vehicle: a Land Rover Discovery. Not a machine I have much respect for normally, Land Rovers and other four-wheel drives appear to be more of a status symbol than a practical tool, a feature of happy, stress-free middle-class existences, and seeing nothing like the challenging mountain roads you see in the adverts. You may wonder why on earth people in bland suburbia have such massive machines – but then again, I suppose, how else are you going to do the school run or get to Sainsbury's supermarket on a Saturday without appearing ordinary?

Kieran's Land Rover, however, was loaded with our gear

and set for a purpose more appropriate to its capabilities – the mean roads of Albania. And so off we went, a day late, our first leg being a four-hour sail to Ostende in Belgium. Our ship was a freight vessel, whose usual customers were overweight haulage drivers, and on which Kieran was regularly able to wangle a good discount for the charity.

The staff we met onboard the ferry, curiously, were all Bosnians, who were pleasantly impressed when I greeted and thanked them in my rudimentary Serbo-Croat.

During our 2001 adventure Niall and I had picked up more than a few phrases in Croatia, a country we spent around three weeks in. We'd also stayed in Bosnia and Montenegro, where much the same language was spoken.

We'd made as much effort as we could on our travels to learn a few basic phrases of each language we encountered over those four months, and even though English – and French and German, which I spoke a little – were widely understood, it was amazing how pleased people in shops, bars or tourist information centres would be to hear us say 'hello', 'goodbye', 'please', 'thank you' or 'excuse me, do you speak English?' in their own tongue.

The exception was Hungarian, a language unrelated to any other and widely accepted to be one of Europe's most difficult to learn. In a Budapest pub, a patient barman spent several minutes slowly going over the phrase 'two large beers, please' with us both, but we just could not get our heads or tongues around it. How Hungarians manage to speak the language so well, I have no idea.

In Serbo-Croat speaking countries, meanwhile, we'd bene-fited from not only around a month's exposure to the language and from a certain logicality in its construction, but also several chance encounters with locals who were happy to teach us new phrases that helped us out no end when negotiat-ing accommodation or travel tickets. We even learned how to count to one hundred, sing 'happy birthday' and swear with reasonable proficiency.

A good deal of that ability (quickly lost, of course, as we arrived in mullet-infested Shkodra and had to switch to reliance on the Albanian section of our phrase book and a few phrases I remembered from Kosovo) was thanks to a young guy called Ivan we met in the Croatian capital, Zagreb. We'd been sitting one evening on the main square, watching the world go by, when he approached us and said something we didn't catch. We explained in Croatian that we didn't understand – and did he speak English? He did indeed, and spoke it very well in fact, expressing his surprise that we spoke so many words of his own language. We got talking further.

Ivan was on his year of compulsory military service, and came from a city an overnight train journey away on the Croatian coast. He explained he was struggling with a heroin addiction, and admitted that when he first approached us he was actually asking us whether we knew where he could get any drugs. Finding army life very difficult, he was absconding and was about to head home to get help.

Finding him to be intelligent, brilliantly witty and heart-wrenchingly honest about his addiction, Niall and I took him under our wing for the few hours before his train home, jokingly forgiving him for thinking we looked like the sorts of people who'd know where to find drugs. We took him out for a pizza and talked about everything from Scottish football to Croatia's war of independence in the early 1990s – and of course the phrases of the local language we'd found ourselves wishing we'd known, which Ivan gladly helped us out with.

A few days later, we visited Ivan in his home town and met his friends, who thanked us profusely for looking after him that night in Zagreb. They hung out with us, showed us around, and of course helped expand our command of Serbo-Croat, including some pretty colourful phrases that I'll not repeat here.

I say Serbo-Croat, but few speakers of the language actually called it that then, and even fewer do so these days. Since the collapse of Yugoslavia and the rise of cultural nationalism in its newly-independent successor states, what was previously the biggest language of Yugoslavia is now generally called Serbian, Croatian or Bosnian, depending on what country you're in – despite the fact that they remain almost entirely mutually intelligible.

Besides practising my Bosnian on the ferry crew, I spent most of the crossing from England to Belgium wondering if now would be a good time to tell Kieran and Peat of my ulterior motive for coming on the journey; but thought that ending up at the bottom of the English Channel with weights tied to my feet might not be the most auspicious beginning to the adventure.

However, I was distracted from these thoughts by the sight of Belgium from the deck – a long, flat landscape broken only by rectangular tower blocks. From the outside, this was not a pretty country, and I wondered how the Belgians coped without panoramic mountain sunsets, and how their economy coped without legions of immaculately-equipped mountaineering, backpacking Germans or overweight ancestor-hunting Americans sporting Royal and Ancient baseball caps.

Once we hit the road in Belgium, we finally felt we were on our way to Albania. The sun was shining, the roads were fast, smooth and flat, and the three of us began making rapid progress, heading through Belgium and the blink-and-you-miss-it countryside of Luxembourg. By the second day of our trip we were deep into Germany.

As we travelled south, Peat told us more about himself, and his contacts in Albania who we were resting much of our journey's hopes on. He had worked a couple of years previously for UNICEF, he explained, on a project that involved teaching children in a slum district of the capital, Tirana, about the dangers of weapons. As a clown and entertainer with a love of children, and as a former soldier in the British Army, Peat was ideal for this work, and he said that as he spoke very little

Albanian, the international language of clowning was put to regular use.

Albania had had a turbulent recent history. It had been ruled for decades by the isolationist dictator Enver Hoxha, and when Communism fell a terrible economic crisis followed when a huge pyramid investment scheme collapsed. Thousands of people were stripped of their savings. The emerging democratic government crumbled, unable to pay wages. The country was overcome by looting, rioting, indiscriminate violence, and the complete breakdown of public institutions, the rule of law, and most alarmingly the armed forces. Anarchy reigned. By the mid 1990s, guns were everywhere in Albania, and when the war in neighbouring Kosovo sent thousands of ethnic Albanian refugees fleeing into the country, the border area was mined by Serbian forces.

Kieran and I saw those mines close up in 1999 on our way home from Kosovo. Just short of the border between Kosovo and Albania – not long before the ill-fated driveshaft incident – we pulled over at the side of the road for a rest. It was a scenic spot. There were green hills on one side of the road, and a field leading down to a pretty lake on the other.

A teenaged boy approached us, and through our rudimentary Albanian and his patchy English we got talking, Kieran and I explaining we were with a charity. We'd found that simply by virtue of being westerners, and especially because we were a humanitarian organisation, the Albanian Kosovans would eagerly open up to us about their experiences of the war and show us their ruined houses, urging us to tell their stories to people back home.

This boy was no different, but he didn't need to tell us much. What he showed us told enough of a story: the field was littered with anti-tank mines. He explained that this was where the border had been mined, even across the bottom of the lake.

The lad took us for a walk through the minefield to show us more.

I should add that anti-tank mines – or at least these ones –

were big things, around half a metre square, perhaps the size of a wheelie bin lid. The grass in the field was very sparse and patchy in the summer heat so it was incredibly easy to spot the mines, but nevertheless we stuck to the precise path the boy led us on.

The mines were made of plastic, and had a small circle in the middle which was the trigger, and there was some language printed in the Cyrillic script – presumably Serbian or Russian. The boy explained that because they were designed for heavy tanks, a human walking over them was probably not enough to set them off. We didn't ask if he'd tried.

Walking through a minefield was probably something you could argue was a reckless thing to do. However, the kid seemed to know exactly what he was doing, and after a few weeks in Kosovo we had just learned to take circumstances in our stride. We'd seen some pretty horrific things on our trip, one or two of which were so horrific I'll rather not detail them here. Everywhere we went, people had fearful stories to recount and evidence to show us of what had happened to them, their families and communities during the months of conflict. To be honest, very little in life shocks or surprises me any more after that.

On one occasion, even, we witnessed an explosion. We were having a coffee with a contact by the riverside in Mitrovica, a city that was previously mixed but which had become starkly divided along ethnic lines during the war. At the time of writing it still remains under close international observation. We were sitting on what had become the Albanian side of the river when, about fifty metres away from us, a shell exploded, fired from the other side. There was mild panic, screaming. People running both away from and towards the site of the explosion. It was not a major incident, though, and nobody seemed to have been injured, the blast ostensibly designed to scare and intimidate more than anything else. Within a few minutes, people were back to their coffees and life had returned to normal.

Or as normal as it could be in those days.

I digress.

Overwhelmed with refugees, landmines, guns and poverty, and devoid of central control, Albania in the mid to late 1990s was generally regarded as one of the most dangerous places on earth.

Into this stepped Peat, his project aiming to educate children about guns, mines and the phenomenal strength of organised crime. It was sad, he commented, that the mafia were the only thing that came close to an authority in the country. Thanks to the prevalence of weapons and the absence of an effective government, Albanian mafia gangs were incredibly powerful. Indeed, I'd heard rumours that it was now Albanians who were at the heart of organised crime in parts of Italy and even as far away as London.

The seriousness of the situation was impressed upon Peat when he first inspected his digs in a run-down, Spartan tower block in the middle of Tirana, and found an old machine gun in his wardrobe. No Gideon Bibles in this part of the world.

After just a few days of working in his particular district of the city, getting to know the children, entertaining them with his magic tricks, and telling them why weapons were dangerous and why crime was no career, there was a knock on his door late at night.

'I knew exactly who it was before I answered,' said Peat. 'I was terrified. I opened the door. You could tell they were the mafia because they were wearing immaculate suits, and even though it was dark they all had sunglasses on. I let them in, convinced this was the end.

'What appeared to be the boss guy sat down, and the others stood over me. Unbelievably, the first thing they said was 'thank you for what you're doing'! They explained that just because they were criminals, it didn't mean they wanted their children to get embroiled in that world too. I couldn't believe it

– they actually supported the anti-mafia project! They began telling me about individual kids I was working with, and how such and such's uncle had been killed in the past, another kid's grandfather had been injured by someone else, and various kids' dads had been shot. They gave me real examples of how crime was ruining the community, and wanted me to make the kids understand that it was their lives, their families, their neighbours who were devastated by it.'

Peat didn't die that night, and he continued for many more weeks in Tirana, working with the kids, drinking Turkish coffee and Albanian cognac in cafés, and getting on like a house on fire with the local councillor for the area, a man named Fatmir, whom Peat was keen to track down again.

Kieran, Peat and I were sitting at a picnic table outside a motorway service station in the north of Italy. We were only around three days' drive into our journey but had made good progress thanks to the fast German autobahns and the fact that we were no longer in an elderly vehicle that was prone to breaking down every five minutes.

Our progress from this point on was going to be a bit slower, as we were about to take on the windy, mountainous roads of the Croatian coastline, congested with German tourists in search of sunshine and cheap beer; so we relaxed in the warm evening sunshine, cold Italian beers going down a treat.

One thing I found odd about continental service stations, at least in this part of the world, was that they had bars. I tried not to think about what chaos would ensue on Britain's roads if the authorities permitted them here.

I began to wonder whether this was the time to come clean, to be honest about my real reasons for coming on the convoy to Albania: to find a little village called Mullet. The three of us were getting on well as a team – Peat seemed a laid back fellow, and Kieran was the adventurous type who liked to mix his serious and hard-working attitude to aid work with an ability to have fun while doing it.

The conversation came to a natural lull. I took a big swig of my Nastro Azurro and cleared my throat.

'Er . . . guys,' I began hesitantly. 'I have to be frank with you both. I know this is going to be a worthwhile convoy and it will do lots of good, but I must admit I have a bit of an ulterior motive for coming to Albania.'

'To find a nice Albanian woman?' suggested Kieran, with such enthusiasm at the idea that I almost wondered whether this had been his motivation for his aid work all along. Although he had a point. Albanian women were certainly beautiful.

'No . . . much more unsexy than that, I'm afraid', I said. 'There's somewhere in Albania I would like to visit. A village called Mullet.'

Kieran and Peat looked at me blankly.

'It's near Tirana apparently, and is where the founder of the city was born. I'd like to go there because I am trying to visit all the places in the world with the word 'mullet' in their name.'

Bewilderment, surprise and perhaps a dose of fear wrestled for supremacy on my travel companions' faces. I couldn't tell whether they thought I was quite insane or just having a laugh. To be honest, at that precise moment, I didn't know which I was either.

After a couple of seconds' silence, they both burst into laughter.

'Really? When did this start?' Kieran asked.

'Just a few months ago. I've found one in Ireland, one in the Caribbean and one in Australia. There may be more, I'm not sure, but I'm going to visit them all.'

I explained as much as I knew about Mullet and its location. And if we could do a little detour on our way home, I suggested, I'd be very grateful.

Thankfully, both Kieran and Peat thought it was a hysterical idea. Completely stupid, but hysterical, and they were both well up for a visit to a village about which we knew nothing except that it shared its name with a hair style popular with 1980s rock stars.

Our journey took us southwards, through the mountains and lakes of Slovenia and along the long coastline of Croatia. It was late July, and the temperatures were in the high 30s for most of the daytime; the heat was unbearable. However, the beautiful blue sea between the coast and lush forested islands, the pretty towns and villages we went through, the imposing mountains through which we drove, and the frequent sight of beautiful Croatian girls wearing not very much, all more than made up for it.

It was slow going, though, with what felt like days on the road punctuated by late afternoons spent on beaches where we might relax over a beer, Kieran and I watching Peat busk with his box of magic tricks for delighted tourists. We soon made it to Montenegro, barely four days after leaving England. Montenegro was the last former Yugoslav republic still to be in political union with Serbia, and the final country on our journey before crossing over into Albania.

Having travelled this way on my journey with Niall two years previously, just before discovering the follicular gem of Shkodra, I recommended to Kieran and Peat that we stop in the Montenegrin town of Kotor, a beautiful old town nestled between steep mountains and a large bay. The bay was technically the sea, but the coastline zig-zagged in on itself for miles in either direction from Kotor, such that we were actually very far inland from the open sea. This made Kotor a great natural harbour, and the mazy, medieval heart of the town was a popular haunt for tourists, mostly from land-locked Serbia and other parts of Montenegro.

It was relatively late in the afternoon when we arrived, the sun already set behind the imposing barrier of the dark mountains that gave Montenegro its name. After parking up on the outskirts of Kotor, we headed off to explore, and had a meal in a pizzeria in the heart of the old town. In amongst the tightly-packed old buildings with ornate exteriors facing on to small, quaint squares, there were plenty packed bars and clubs, pounding out thumping dance music and giving the town a youthful, vibrant atmosphere that seemed surprising for what I suppose was in effect the Blackpool of Yugoslavia.

After eating, Peat took his hamper of tricks to go find a good spot to busk, while I offered to show Kieran round as much of the old town as I could remember from my previous visit with Niall. Not having the best orientation skills in the world, I got us both quite lost, and we ended up returning to the main gates of the old town later than we'd agreed with Peat.

No worries on that count, however, because Peat was absolutely fine on his own, and we found him surrounded by a large cheering and laughing crowd. He was playing a penny whistle, which was clutched between his teeth and pointed upwards with a puppet balanced on the other end, while simultaneously he juggled four clubs. The applause ended long after his gracious bow, and Kieran and I stood at the back, no less impressed at Peat's skills than when we first experienced his ping-pong spewing at Gatwick airport.

After a night's camping under the stars on the edge of the town, we got moving early. This was for three reasons. Firstly, we still had a few hours' journey before we could cross the border, head through the north of Albania, and reach Tirana, our final destination. Secondly, as soon as the sun peeped over the horizon, the temperature flicked back from 'mountain chill' to 'desert scorch'. Thirdly, and most definitively, it is very hard to contemplate having a lazy morning when you wake up to discover your sleeping bag is crawling with ants.

THREE

Kanun

Albania is an amazing country and will always be one of my favourite places on earth. It is wild, mountainous, dusty, and steeped in the traditions of family and clan honour, especially in the more sparsely populated north. Traces of previous occupiers and political influences can be found throughout the country, including Roman ruins and Turkish food from past history, and from early 20th century Italian architecture to Communist-era Chinese tractors.

Traditionally, life in Albania had been governed by the *Kanun*, a collection of centuries-old laws which regulated working and family life. Although largely suppressed under Communism, it remained influential in many parts of the country and enjoyed a resurgence in the 1990s after the collapse of central government and the state's control over people's daily lives.

The *Kanun*'s guiding principle was honour – everything you did was to protect and enhance your family's name. This had both positive and negative consequences.

On the one hand, the concept of *besa* instilled a duty to show the utmost hospitality to visitors, on the reasoning that your home belonged firstly to God, secondly to any guests, and only thirdly to yourself. Your guest was to be treated with the greatest respect, and any harm that came to them while they were receiving your hospitality would be your responsibility and a great stain on your family honour.

A more sinister manifestation was *gjakmarrja*, or blood feud. According to the *Kanun*, if someone is harmed in your family, it was your right – and indeed duty – to maintain your family honour by taking revenge. Often such tit-for-tat feuds would last for several generations, and with the return of the *Kanun* as a social code after Communism, blood feuds re-emerged too. I read stories of feuds that would see male members of the family (in misogynistic Albania, women did not count in such situations) living as prisoners in their own home because their family was 'in blood' with another family.

Communism had generally minimised much of the *Kanun*'s influence, and instead imposed itself on Albanian society in other ways. Towns across the beautiful, rugged countryside, even in very rural areas, were dominated by tall, bland tower blocks; while all across the country, particularly near borders, you could find small, hemispherical concrete bunkers in the ground.

These bunkers were a fascinating testament to the paranoid leadership of Enver Hoxha. Other than a brief alignment with Maoist China, Albania was isolated ideologically from all other countries, including other Communist powers, and Hoxha believed that Albania had to protect itself from imminent invasion from possibly any direction – Italy, the UK, the USA, Yugoslavia, even the Soviet Union. And so throughout Albania these bunkers were built, littering the countryside. They were solid shells of dense concrete with a slit on one side and an interior just big enough for a couple of men and a machine gun. Facing the borders, these bunkers would be the main line of defence in the face of an invasion which of course never came.

After the fall of Communism, the virtually indestructible bunkers could not easily be removed, and continue to this day to dot the countryside, often painted in bright, attractive colours.

Our intended destination, and Peat's old haunt, was a slum suburb of Tirana called Bathore. Built on the site of a Communist-era state-run farm, it was settled and built on after the fall of Communism by a group of migrants escaping the poverty and lawlessness of the north of Albania. Because the settlement did not officially exist, and also no doubt due to the generally poor state of public services in the country, it was never formally connected up to the electricity and water networks. Over time, it did acquire a sporadic and probably less than legal electricity connection, but the residents still had to take containers to neighbouring suburbs each day to get water.

We arrived in Bathore despite Peat struggling to fully remember the directions. Tirana was a busy and congested city where driving was a perilous occupation and roads frequently lacked helpful features such as signposts or smooth surfaces. However things got familiar to Peat as we drew close, and eventually we arrived.

Bathore was a fairly ramshackle collection of houses, built to varying quality, with rough roads and pathways that the Land Rover shuddered and jolted along. We soon made it to Fatmir the local councillor's house.

It was a pleasant dwelling, and probably among the nicer ones in the district, although that wasn't saying a lot. A single storey building made of stone and concrete, and with an open courtyard at the back, it faced a dusty road on which a crowd of curious children were already gathering.

Fatmir was expecting us. Peat had called a couple of days previously from Montenegro, a conversation that can't have been the smoothest given that Peat's Albanian and Fatmir's English were both pretty negligible. A common language hadn't impeded their friendship, however, and they greeted each other with warm handshakes and embraces. Kieran and I were enthusiastically welcomed too.

Outside Fatmir's house on the road were a couple of tables and chairs. Fatmir gestured to us to sit down, and moments later we were drinking very welcome ice cold beers.

'Gazur!' said Fatmir, raising his bottle of beer. We toasted back, and glugged away the heat and the dust. We'd barely arrived, and we were on the beer already. Fatmir clearly had his priorities right.

As we sat, the crowd of children who had greeted our arrival in the Land Rover stayed with us, staring at us with bold eyes as if we'd jetpacked into Bathore from an alternative dimension. Which in many ways, I suppose, we had: this was a culture, a language, a people, and above all a poverty that was a world away from what I knew back in Inverness.

While the children seemed to be all ages up to adolescence, the younger ones were much less inhibited about talking to us in rapid Albanian and finding no more common ground with us than the exchange of a few names.

Communication became easier however with the arrival of a girl called Albana, a student at the University of Tirana who lived in Bathore and spoke fluent English. Fatmir had sent someone to get her, figuring we could use a translator during our stay. There had been a few aid agencies and other visitors in the area in the past, she explained, and Fatmir usually called on her to help with communication.

Through our newly-acquired interpreter, Fatmir got down to business and we were able to find out a little bit more about our immediate surroundings. Bathore was divided into a number of sectors, he explained, for one of which he was the local councillor. Things were difficult for folk in Bathore not only with the poor electricity and water situation, but also the cramped housing conditions and very high unemployment.

Fatmir himself was an electrician by trade, but had not been in work for several months. This was difficult for him with a wife – whom we had met briefly whom we would rarely see out of the kitchen during our visit – and three young children. He made a very small income from the bar he ran out of his house, the patio of which we were sitting on. There men would gather, often in the early morning, to catch up on the news over a coffee or an early morning shot of raki, the national spirit made from distilled grapes.

His political and practical skills had collided rather unfortunately for him just the other day, he explained, pointing to a nasty scar above one of his eyes. He had recently redirected the electricity supply of a man in the area to a family he'd judged to have more need, and had been attacked for his troubles by the disgruntled constituent. Clearly with so little resources, politics was an especially difficult business around here.

The main challenge for the district was getting a well dug for drinking water. There had been various projects with which they had received help, such as a school and a clinic, which Fatmir promised to show us around the next day. But the water situation was dire – people had to take containers to neighbouring parts of Tirana. Indeed, as we sat talking, various convoys of women and children with armfuls and wheelbarrowfuls of jerry cans and plastic containers had been passing by. Fatmir explained that they had rough plans of how and where to build the well – they just needed the money to do it.

As we sat outside Fatmir's house talking and getting to know our hosts, something unexpected happened. A young bearded guy approached us in a Fulham Football Club t-shirt.

'Awright, what's 'appnin?'

Din was Albanian, from Bathore, but had very recently returned from four years in London where he had lived and worked with his brother who was a waiter in a restaurant. Having been away until just a matter of weeks ago, and still readjusting to life back in Albania, his Cockney was straight out of *EastEnders*.

We introduced ourselves to Din, explaining our visit and Peat's connections. He seemed delighted to meet us, and offered to help show us around and look after us during our stay.

Kieran, Peat and I were to be staying in Fatmir's house, at his insistence. We had offered to sleep in the Land Rover, which came armed with a fantastic extendable tent on the roof, and

Peat also had brought a tent, so we had got well used to sleeping in them on the journey so far. Fatmir, though, would hear nothing of it. In the true spirit of Albanian hospitality, we ended up being given a room to sleep in that we suspected from the large bed and sofas was actually that of Fatmir and his wife.

The hospitality, despite the poverty of our hosts, was humbling. We ate a hearty meal of vegetables and rice, with an obligatory raki to follow, and with the day drawing to a close, we turned in.

I lay in bed reflecting on the journey so far. It was brilliant to be back in Albania. I had loved my two previous trips there, and had always wanted to come back. The mountains were as beautiful, the city as chaotic, and the people as wonderful as I had remembered. But of course the country was not perfect. There were clear social and economic needs. People were struggling to make a living. And the misogynistic side of Albania's very conservative culture seemed unjust – women were for kitchens, child-rearing and getting water, and ostensibly not much else.

But I wasn't here to judge, I told myself. I was here to learn, listen and hopefully help.

Oh yes, and visit a place that shared a name with a haircut.

The next couple of days involved finding out more about Bathore, taking a tour of the suburb, meeting more people, and talking with Fatmir, Albana, Din and others about the challenges that lay ahead for the community.

Fatmir took us to the local school, a large new building that had recently been built with the help of a humanitarian organisation. It was great that they had a school, he insisted, but funding for equipment was next to nothing, and paying teachers' wages was very difficult.

The same was the case with Bathore's clinic. It was structurally in good shape but, as the doctor was eager to show us, lacking in much more than the most basic of equipment.

Before our departure, Kieran had raided his charity's stores for anything vaguely medical that had been donated recently, and the doctor was chuffed to receive a variety of supplies including syringes, needles, cotton wool and one or two second-hand but fully-functioning pieces of medical equipment.

While sitting outside Fatmir's house the same evening making balloon animals for the omnipresent crowd of children, Peat recalled the severity of the medical situation on his previous visit. Then, he had been doing some circus performing for the kids one afternoon when a nurse from the clinic had come over and without saying a word simply walked off with his large box of balloons.

Feeling not a little put out by this, he went after her to challenge her. The nurse simply reached into the box and pulled a balloon out.

'This,' she had said to Peat in a terse tone, 'is a tourniquet.' She fished out another. 'This one will tie a splint.' And another. 'This one will be attached to a syringe and be a drip.' And so on though a catalogue of improvised medical tools, until she walked off into the medical centre, leaving Peat feeling very embarrassed.

'I was astounded,' he told us. 'The state of the clinic was so poor that things I'd been using to make blow-up dogs, hats, giraffes and swords, were valuable to them to save people's lives. I wondered whether what I was doing in the way of circus skills and entertainment was frivolous, but I know it raises a smile and that's something far too lacking in so many parts of the world.'

Indeed, some months after our Albanian visit, Peat went on tour with a circus around Israel and the Palestinian territories. In one Palestinian refugee camp, he explained in an email, he had been performing magic tricks and playing parachute games with children one day, until he noticed an old man crying at the edge of the space they were using. The man told him he was crying with delight because it was the first time in years he had seen any children laughing.

'That was when I knew that the work I was doing was important,' Peat wrote – and it certainly was that dusty summer in Bathore. If nothing else, we, and particularly Peat, brought smiles and laughter.

We spent a total of three days in Bathore, meeting people and learning about life in the area. We were welcomed into people's houses, tiny cramped buildings made with rudimentary building materials. It seemed that pretty much nothing was wasted, and even part of the wall between Fatmir's house and his neighbour's was built with old car doors. I almost laughed at the thought of going across the garden, winding down the window and having a good natter with next door.

Sanitation was a problem too. Fatmir had a basic outdoor toilet next to his house, but even then compared to others in the area he was lucky. I remember one woman showing us around her house with what was almost a nervous shame, showing us where her family of ten would live and sleep, in a space the size of my own flat back in Inverness.

We spoke with the men in the village – it was always the men – about the wider economic situation and the future, usually over a stomach-churning 8am glass of raki. We were told about how they had hopes and dreams that their children would be educated and be able to get a better life. Most people under Communism had not been able to get much education, but now with freedom and democracy, they explained, they could try to scrape together the money to keep them in school, and perhaps even go abroad to work.

It seemed to be a common theme, going abroad. Such was the state of the country and the lack of job opportunities that emigration was often one of the best options. Din's brother had done it for example. We asked Din and Albana if that was on their agendas.

'Nah mate,' Din had replied. He explained he had hope for the future and wanted to stay in Albania. He did not know what he could do, but hoped to find work. Albana, meanwhile, was happy to be able to go to university where she studied economics and hoped that she would find a decent job at the end of it. She was an intelligent, warm-hearted person, whose translation had been a lifeline for us, and which had been delivered with an unflappable and nearly flawless English, despite the constant demands that simultaneous translation placed on her. It was encouraging to think that the future of Albania lay in the hands of fine young folk like her and Din.

It was inspiring to hear of the hope the people in Bathore had. They were among the poorest people in an impoverished corner of Europe, but they dreamed, they aspired.

The day we left, our heads and notebooks full of information, Fatmir and Albana wanted to take us to the national museum, which sat proudly on Skanderbeg Square in the heart of Tirana. An uncompromising testament to Communist architecture, the museum was a simple and ugly square concrete block. It was livened up only by a vast mural on the front. This depicted a massed crowd of the proletariat, farming implements and rifles in hands, marching forwards together and led by a determined looking woman clutching the national flag, a black, two-headed eagle on a red background. Girl power, Albanian-style. I'd seen and admired the building on my two previous visits, and had always wondered what it was like inside.

The interior contained a sparse but relatively well-ordered and well-maintained collection of artefacts and interpretations of Albanian history; a history which is nothing if not eventful. A tiny country but with some considerable strategic importance, it boasts some beautiful Roman ruins in the south, and in more recent eras has been invaded by, occupied by and at war with more or less all of its near neighbours, including hundreds of years as a part of the Ottoman Empire.

The museum had fascinating descriptions, collections and first-hand accounts of Albania under Communism and during the two world wars. It was moving and not a little inspiring to see a small country that had so little survive such hardship and still have a sense of national pride.

Not far from my mind, however, was Mullet. Would I find any clues about its precise location, its history, its . . . haircuts? I realised that on our last day in Tirana I still didn't know anything about Mullet. We were leaving soon – I had to find something quickly. Tirana was absent from many of the early maps in the museums – Roman, Middle Ages or Ottoman. It was strange to think that a capital would be created as late as the 1600s in a European country that had such a long history.

I mentioned this casually to Albana.

'Strange how Tirana was such a relatively recent creation. I remember reading . . . er, somewhere . . . that it was created by a guy in the 17th century.'

'Yes, that's right,' she replied, giving me only half her attention while also being absorbed in the artefacts herself.

'I remember reading somewhere that the guy who founded it came from a place called Mullet. Do you . . .?'

'Yes, now come look at this,' she interrupted eagerly, 'We've reached the Second World War.'

Maybe Mullet was a national secret, or a source of shame to Albanians. Given most mullet haircuts, I couldn't blame them.

We ended up finishing the museum within a couple of hours, and while it was an interesting lesson and a fascinating adventure to see inside the imposing building, I did feel a little deflated not discovering more about Mullet and its famous inhabitant . . . and more's the pity, it was time for us to go.

We stepped outside, Kieran, Peat and I being almost knocked over by what had over the course of the morning become a thumping midday heat. We covered our eyes after the gloom of the largely windowless museum, Fatmir and Albana sauntering after us unfazed by the scorching sunshine.

The heat had been a major battle for us in Albania, and I had especially struggled in the temperatures of over thirty degrees Celsius. Of course, I'm never good in heat at the best of times, but in hot, dusty conditions with minimal washing facilities, I had really found it difficult. With the dirt, sweat and grime I was oozing, I had looked a state since arriving in Tirana, and often felt very pathetic and incompetent when our Albanian friends, for all their poverty and few clothes, were still neat, dignified and, more often than not, extremely elegant in their appearance.

Anyway, it was time to bid our farewells, and before we did so we went to a newspaper kiosk to buy a map of Albania. It would be a good souvenir and would help us track down Mullet. We bought it and the three of us pored over it. The map was bright and colourful, with each of the provinces clearly marked in a different shade.

We looked near Tirana for a sign of Mullet. Nothing. Except . . . just to the north, perhaps by an hour or so . . . Milot.

Not Mullet. Milot.

'Bugger.' Was just about all I could manage.

'That could still be it – it could be a spelling mistake,' said Kieran, after a moment's silence. He had a point. The Albanian language was a funny one – its complicated grammar meant that sometimes a name or placename could change in spelling slightly, depending on where it sat in the sentence. I didn't quite understand, but it was something to do with what case the noun was – it could be dative, nominative, retentive, or probably numerous others I'd never heard of. Tirana, for example, could be written as either Tirana, Tiranë or Tiranës in different situations. It could easily have been that Milot changed to Mullet depending on, well, I don't know, whether you were left or right-handed, how many people you were talking to, what colour t-shirt you were wearing, or what the temperature was outside.

'We could still visit it,' suggested Peat helpfully. 'It's on our way home after all.'

'Yes, but . . . it's not Mullet. It's Milot. Milot is not a bloody haircut,' I snapped. 'We've travelled all the way out here on the basis of a wrong spelling. If it was actually called Mullet, it would be on the map as Mullet. And there's no Mullet on this map.' I punched the map in frustration.

Fatmir and Albana wondered over to see what we were talking about.

'What's wrong?' asked Albana.

'Nothing,' replied Kieran cheerfully. 'We're just checking the route for the best way home!'

And so after our fond farewells to our kind and generous hosts, the three of us walked back to the Land Rover, and headed off. North. Homewards.

Via bloody Milot.

We drove north, determined to be over the border and back into Montenegro by nightfall. We headed out of the city in relative silence, Peat and Kieran attempting to cheer me up, but I was having none of it.

Various thoughts sprung to mind. First, how could I have been so stupid as to not actually check what the damn place was called? The websites I'd found references to Mullet in were either those of western aid agencies, or scrappily-translated Albanian tourist sites. It was perfectly feasible, therefore, that a mistaken, English translation of the name could have been used. Why had I not checked this out first?

On the other hand, though, did any of this matter? I'd had a really enjoyable journey with two great people, and we'd hopefully done a lot of good work in Bathore. It was only the beginning, we intended, and perhaps more could be done for the community there in the future. Was it not an insult to them that I was more angry about my stupid mullet project, than the poverty their lives were dogged by? Had I not abused Kieran and Peat's trust by having this as my main motivation above humanitarian compassion?

I didn't know what to think. I was annoyed and upset. This was the first step on my mullet adventure and I'd failed most spectacularly.

After a while we came to the sign announcing we were entering the district of Milot.

'Photo time,' said Kieran brightly.

'You got your camera?'

'It's called bloody Milot,' I replied huffily, like a spoilt child. 'Don't bother.'

I was sitting in the back seat feeling very sorry for myself.

We drove on, but a few moments after when the sign came up signalling the turn-off to the village itself, Kieran pulled over. He wasn't taking no for an answer.

'Come on,' he said. 'You've travelled across Europe to do this. Just one photo. It won't take a moment.'

I sighed, shuffled out, stood under the roadsign, and Kieran took a photo. Of me.

Standing under a road sign.

Which announced the turn-off to an Albanian village.

Called Milot.

Not Mullet.

We got back in and drove off again.

It was a very, very long journey home.

FOUR

The Mullet, the Skullet and the Femme Mullée

Back in Inverness, the weeks after Albania were not easy. I was wracked with doubts and confusion – had it been the right thing to do? Had it been out of order to trivialise a humanitarian aid trip? Was the mission worth pursuing, after I'd failed at the first hurdle? More fundamentally, how stupid had I been, to go to a village on the other side of Europe, only to find that in its native language it was spelt differently from the English?

I was a fool. Some of my friends didn't help, either. Most of my friends back in Aberdeen knew what I had done, and one friend Mark texted me one evening to taunt me about my failure.

'I have a gift for you! It is a blond mullet wig. Whenever you visit a mullet you must wear it at all times.'

Mark was a keen birdwatcher. A chef by trade, he had got sick of shouting for a living, and had slowly spent more time birdwatching, something the countryside around Aberdeen offered in abundance. He did a variety of work for conservation groups, and in effect was paid to fly around the north of Scotland counting birds out of the window of a small plane, or to spend days or weeks on end camping out in remote corners of Shetland or on North Sea oilrigs with only his binoculars and a notepad for company. He loved it, and was very proud of the fact that he could state his occupation as the rather wonderful 'freelance ornithologist'.

Why should I wear a mullet wig? Was I some sort of novelty

item, some sort of crackpot eccentric? What on earth was Mark doing with one, anyway?

I hated mullets. They were ugly, repulsive haircuts worn by white trailer trash in the USA and young trendy types in the UK who actually weren't trendy at all. Just because I had chosen to visit every place in the world with 'mullet' in its name didn't mean I had to get quite so close to my subject. It was like the criminal psychologist, I reasoned, who studied, observed and explained criminals, but did not actually become one himself.

I transferred the same logic to Mark's hobby and texted him back: 'Only if you go out bird-watching covered in feathers and wearing a large beak.'

Within a minute, there was a beep beep in response: 'Ungrateful sod!'

Honestly. Some people just didn't understand.

Niall, however, was a bit more reasonable.

I emailed him in South Korea to let him know how Albania had gone. Niall seemed to be getting on very well, after life in the castle. He had changed from living a life of either working as a kitchen porter or getting wasted at parties, to one of calmness, discipline and academic rigour. He was enjoying teaching English, mostly to young primary-age children, and had been studying the Korean language intently. He had even started to learn Russian in his spare time.

Niall was surprised that I had actually gone ahead with my quest in Albania, but disputed my claim that it was a wasted trip. He wrote in an email:

Does the place name need to have the exact word 'mullet' within it? How about Mul-let? And what about places with a different alphabet and non-precise transcriptions. In Russian, which is mostly phonetic, any English version would look like Mulet or most likely something else as the 'uh' sound of the letter u doesn't really exist there. Likewise in Korean, the closest theoretical transcription would be 'Meol-let' where the 'eo' is kind of between an 'uh' and an 'oh'. How about 'Mullet' if the u has an 'oo' sound? Also, finally, why didn't the Albanian mullet count? I thought that was the mightiest of all mullet towns.

I replied:

It doesn't count, because the word 'mullet' isn't contained within the word. If somewhere in, for example, Russia or Korea, there was something that translated as Meol-let then it wouldn't count. This is why Mullet in Albania didn't count because the Albanian spelling was actually Milot. Mullet was only on English language websites and therefore isn't the 'proper' name of the place. Mulet certainly wouldn't count.I've got rules, you see. I can't just go visiting places that *sound like* 'mullet'. That would be silly.

Niall's response was quick and to the point:

Does that mean that if you were, for example, a collector of towns called 'Moscow' you couldn't count the most famous example because the Russian name is Moskva?

That made me think. He had a point. Of course I would visit the Russian capital if I was visiting places called Moscow. It would probably be my first stop, in fact – after the small Ayrshire village of Moscow, at least. Scotland's unique like that – without leaving central Scotland, you can travel between Moscow and California in a matter of minutes. Maybe, then, Milot would still count because its English name was Mullet.

However, I was still not sure. I'd seen reference to 'Mullet' on only two English language websites, the one I had originally read which told me about the foundation of Tirana, and a charity's reference to the Mullet refugee camp. Maybe, I wrote to Niall, Mullet was just some sort of misspelling or a mistranslation. I still had no overwhelming evidence that Mullet was a proper name for it in English.

Niall wasn't giving up, and emailed back with a list of links. He found an online travel guide that made reference to Mullet; an Albanian human rights group's page about the Mullet refugee camp; a news report from an Albanian website which reported on a recent election and quoted an elderly voter from Mullet; and most intriguingly the website of an American television actress who mentioned Mullet on a page about her charity work. All those sites referred to the village as Mullet.

Niall had excelled himself. Not only was he proving almost as keen about the project as me, he'd won me back the one Mullet that I'd bagged. Sure we'd not actually visited it because I was adamant it was spelt wrong, but we'd past the turn-off for it. That counted. Didn't it?

Little did I know at the time that, actually, I had made an even more outrageous mistake with Milot than being confused over its spelling – that, however, is perhaps a story for later.

All that mattered at that point was that it counted. Well, in my mind it did.

From zero, I was back to one again. That was an increase of infinity percent! I could do this, I *knew* I could. I had a great feeling about it. It had been a shaky start, but thanks to Niall's reasoning I was back in business. The project was back on the road!

My searching began again with renewed optimism. Armed with my trusty sidekick, Google, I explored the murky side-streets of the internet for more references to mullet place names around the world. It wasn't easy: most pages were hideously-badly designed tributes to the haircut, complete with shocking photos; recipes for fish dishes involving the red or grey mullet; or mentions of the mullets I already knew about in Albania, Australia, the Caribbean and Ireland.

But I persevered, googling for things like 'mullet placename' or 'mullet location'. I didn't give up on each search until I had checked all the results, often into the twentieth or thirtieth page of search results. And I bet *you've* never checked the thirtieth page of any of your search results. The rampant googling bore fruit – I uncovered Mullet Bay in Florida, USA, and Mullet Creek in Ontario, Canada.

Mullet Bay seemed to be a typical Florida tourist resort, while one of the few references I could find to the Canadian one was a technical report about development charges for storm drainage components. As you can imagine, the report was not a riveting read, and by the end of it I was none the wiser about what development charges for storm drainage components actually were, let alone where exactly Mullet Creek was or how many people lived there.

Not long after moving to Inverness, I'd signed up to an intriguing website that served as a worldwide accommodation exchange network for travellers. The idea was that you created a profile, explaining a little about yourself and what spare accommodation you had, and then people would write to you, introducing themselves and asking to stay. If you liked the sound of them, you'd then put them up for free in your spare bed or sofa for a couple of days and show them a little of your area; and if you didn't like the sound of them you could make your polite excuses and say no. It would work the other way round, too: you'd go travelling to a new place, write to hosts in that part of the world and tell them a little about yourself in the hope that they'd agree to put you up.

It was great fun, and with a small part of me still hankering after the fun of my own travelling days, I found that hosting people from other parts of the world was like travelling by proxy: hearing stories about where people came from and the journeys they were taking helped to scratch my seemingly permanently itchy feet and satisfy my wanderlust when at times all I seemed to do was work hard. One of the best things about hosting people was that in showing them around Inverness I could see my home city through different eyes, seeing what they noticed, comparing impressions, and being not a little proud at their delight in the beauty of the area.

I hosted some fascinating people from many different countries, learning a lot, having a great time, and of course making some great friends.

It was through this website that, later in the year after my Albanian adventure, I hosted a young American student named Mel who was visiting Inverness. Mel was good fun, an amusing, entertaining and well-travelled girl with a strong alternative streak, and we immediately hit it off. She hailed from Washington state in the far north-west of the USA, and lived an hour or two from Seattle. When I explained the mission to her, she laughed, and told me she had another mullet for me – of sorts.

A friend of a friend of hers was a film-maker, and had written and directed a spoof documentary called 'Mulletville' a while back about small-town trailer trash in the USA. He had based the film on two towns near where she lived.

I loved the idea – something that would have a good dig at mullets and those who wore them. I wondered whether Mulletville could count, though. It would be only right that my journey should take in the United States of America, the country that could stake a strong claim for being the home of the mullet. And if I could visit the two villages that inspired the documentary, watch the film, and meet its creator, surely that would collectively mean that in a very real sense I would have visited Mulletville itself?

Mel and I agreed to keep in touch, and so it was that my list gained its first fictitious item.

Besides the search for mullet place names, I continued to spot mullets on heads too. I saw the same few mullets around Inverness, while on trips away for work or to see friends I would engage in some comparative study. Aberdeen, for example, didn't have much more than Inverness's modest show of mulletry, while Edinburgh, with its mix of urbane and hippy populations, was significantly better.

My mulletology moved to a whole new level one evening

late on in the summer. I was sitting in the Harlequin, my local pub, and got talking to three Australians.

Strangely for what turned out to be a pivotal moment, I can't remember why I was out that night, or who was with me. I am sure I must have been there with friends, as I've never really been a solo drinker. Partly it's the fear of spending my whole time there – a fear inspired by the fat, greasy man you see sitting in the corner of most pubs, swarthy-faced with a dinner-stained sweatshirt, nose reddened by a lifetime of alcohol, and whose morose company is only tolerated by the staff because his custom bankrolls their business.

I also don't like drinking alone in pubs because I just don't have the confidence. If I'm meeting a friend and they arrive after me, I find sitting there by myself really awkward in case anyone thinks I'm some sort of saddo destined for a life like . . . well, the fat, greasy man you get sitting in the corner of most pubs. If friends are more than about five minutes late I start texting them and thinking I should tell people sitting near me that I do actually have friends, and they'll be along shortly thank you very much.

So, anyway. I don't remember who I was with because it was the three Australians who stuck in my memory. Or one of them, at least. They were all working in Dornoch, a small town about an hour's drive north of Inverness, which was famous for its golf courses, glorious beaches and a beautiful cathedral which – a couple of years later – was the location of Madonna and Guy Ritchie's wedding. My new acquaintances were all on the usual Australian 'rite of passage' of working in London for a year, going travelling around Europe for a few months, and then returning to a different part of the UK to work some more.

One girl said she was from Queensland.

'Ah, the home of the mullet!' I exclaimed. 'I hear they're really big in that part of the world.'

'Absolutely,' she replied, her face lighting up. 'I see them all the time, it's shocking. It's easily the best place in the world for mullets.'

'Oh, I don't know about that,' I said. 'I went to a town called Shkodra in the north of Albania. That took some beating. There were mullets everywhere.'

'No way,' she challenged. 'When I'm back home, I'm seeing fifteen or sixteen points a day, minimum.' I raised my eyebrow questioningly. At last, someone who was into their mullets, who wanted to talk about them, and even described them as 'shocking'. Plus, it hadn't escaped my attention that she was exceptionally pretty. I was hooked.

'Points?' I asked. 'Points for what?'

'The scoring system!' she replied. 'It's a vital part of mullet-spotting. I give myself one point for a regular male mullet, two points for a skullet, three points for a femme mullée, and four points for a chullet, a child mullet. And as I say – rural Queensland, at least fifteen points a day. Guaranteed.'

'Fantastic!' I declared. 'I must try this!' Child mullets were very rare indeed (and, I thought, what a great word 'chullet' was), and so four points sounded appropriate; meanwhile femme mullées were less rare but unusual enough to warrant three points. As for skullets, male mullets with a receding hairline, they were quite rare too but had a degree of celebrity endorsement, at least in Britain, through the likes of comedian Bill Bailey and children's television presenter Terry Nutkins.

I was all for getting deeper into conversation with her – meeting girls who were mullet experts themselves was a rarity, and ones as pretty as she was on top of that were even rarer. I particularly wanted to ask her if she knew about Mullet Creek in Queensland. Sadly, however, she and her two friends were just about leaving as I had started talking to them, and the other two were keen to get away, somewhat perturbed by the international mulletology convention they'd found themselves drawn into. Presumably they just didn't get mullets like their friend did.

Such a shame – just as I found a mullet-spotting soulmate, just as I encountered someone who was as enthusiastic as me, if not more so, just as I discover a great new scoring system . . .

they were off. I thanked her for the inspiration, and bade her goodbye.

I had a new dimension to my mullet-spotting. How many points could I get in a day I thought? Could I beat fifteen?

What a lovely girl she was.

I never got her name.

The weeks passed, and the nights drew in. Late one night in the middle of Inverness's dark, cold winter, I made a list of all the mullets so far.

Mullet, Albania (visited).
Mullet Bay, St Martin's, Caribbean.
Mullet Creek, Queensland, Australia.
Belmullet, County Mayo, Ireland.
Mullet Bay, Florida, USA.
Mullet Creek, Ontario, Canada.
Mulletville, Washington state (kind of), USA.

Seven mullets. One down, six to go. This was achievable. It was daunting, admittedly – three continents, tens of thousands of miles, and an awful lot of annual leave and savings. But they were only placenames. Spots on our wee planet. Places to go. Boxes to tick.

My eye was particularly drawn to Belmullet. My brother sending me my old English teacher's poetry collection with a poem that referred to the village was almost like fate, as if I was meant to know about Belmullet, meant to visit it. As if it was my destiny. It was only Ireland, not the other side of the world, I told myself – I'd never been, and it would be cheap, quick and easy to get to. Plus of course they spoke English. Of sorts.

I booked the week before the following Easter as leave and began to make plans.

FIVE

The Road to Belmullet

I decided to go to Ireland at Easter time – work would be quiet and I figured it wouldn't be too close to peak tourist season. I was looking forward to seeing it and although it was just over the water from Scotland, I'd never been. I booked a combined train and ferry ticket from Inverness to Belfast, packed a bag, and went.

I suppose I could have flown, but I wanted to be environmentally friendly. Plus, being a Highlander, I'd never been on the train line from Glasgow to Stranraer, the town in the far south-west of Scotland from where the Belfast ferry sailed. In any case, I always find journeys as interesting as destinations, as much a part of a holiday as the time spent in a place.

Trains, particularly, seem fascinating places to meet people. It's probably the sense of confinement that leads people to talk to random strangers so much more easily than they would elsewhere. When I was about eighteen (an alarmingly long time ago, now I think about it), I was on a train from Yorkshire to Aberdeenshire, a journey of something like six or seven hours, and got talking to the woman next to me. She was in late middle-age, and after the usual easy-going pleasantries, she explained she was on the run from her abusive husband. After years of torment she'd finally snapped, and early one morning she'd packed as much as she could carry and jumped on a train to stay with a good friend in Aberdeen.

As tears slowly trickled down her face, her previously composed demeanour disintegrated and she told me stories of the physical and psychological abuse, and her doubts as to whether she was doing the right thing in running away.

Before I got off the train, a couple of stops ahead of her, I made her promise to tell the police.

I often wonder what happened to her.

Abroad, train journeys can seem so much more exciting and exotic than British trains (not to mention cheaper, faster and rather more likely to be on time). Sleeper trains are especially fun, as you depend on the people you travel with to help pass the time when – as is often the case – sleep fails to come.

On our 2001 travels, Niall and I took an overnight train from Sofia in Bulgaria to Bucharest in Romania. With us were two guys – a Finn and an Australian – and an English lass, who we'd all met in our hostel in Sofia and with whom we teamed up for a couple of legs of our journey. At the border, not long after we'd handed our passports over to the Romanians, a border guard entered our compartment.

'Who is the two men with the English passports?' he asked.

Assuming he meant Niall and me, I replied 'those aren't English passports, they're UK passports. And we're Scottish, not English.'

Duly chastised, the official asked Niall and me to disembark with him, whereupon we were taken into separate offices and grilled about our journey so far, presumably to ensure our stories matched up. Or else they were simply intrigued by all the passport stamps we'd made sure we received at each border we crossed.

Not long after, when the train had slowed to another brief halt, an amiable young Romanian guy knocked on the door of our compartment and asked if we knew why we'd stopped. Of course, he knew fine well that we didn't know any more than he did. Before long, though, he was sitting down, chatting to us, and sharing the food he had. Like many of the younger generation in Eastern Europe, he had simply wanted to practise his English on us upon hearing our voices, and of course make his own journey pass more pleasantly.

A common language, though, is certainly no precursor to talking to strangers on trains. Earlier in the trip Niall and I had travelled from Slovenia to Hungary, and found ourselves in a compartment with two middle-aged men. We overcame the communication barrier through pointing, sign language and maps, and when they said they were Bulgarian, we exclaimed 'Illian Kiriakov!', referring to a famous Bulgarian footballer who used to play for Aberdeen. 'Stilian Petrov, Celtic!' they also pointed out, nodding enthusiastically at the common bond we'd developed through Scottish-based Bulgarian footballers.

For the idealists who seek a common tongue for Europe, forget about English or French – surely the best candidate is the international language of football.

My journey to Belfast was no exception to the rule of fun and random encounters – after surviving my three trains to Perth, Glasgow and then Stranraer, I was sitting in the ferry terminal when a familiar face walked in. Mhairi was studying in Glasgow and I knew her through mutual friends. She was heading to Belfast for the weekend for a friend's birthday.

'Come and join us tonight,' she suggested. I loved small world moments like this.

The ferry journey was a little choppy but coming from the Western Isles I was used to ferries. Not that growing up on an island meant I automatically had a good sailor's constitution. A number of gruelling crossings of the Minch had led to occasions when my stomach had turned inside out. This, however, was a much smoother crossing than most I had undertaken, on a much bigger boat.

It was also a novelty not having the safety announcements on the tannoy read out in Gaelic.

At the other end, Mhairi met up with her friends and I headed off to my hostel. Well, I say 'my hostel', but I hadn't actually booked it, I'd just circled it in the Lonely Planet guide to Ireland as one that looked half-decent and not too far away from the ferry terminal. When I got there, however, the man behind the desk puffed out his cheeks and shook his head.

This week, he explained, Belfast was hosting the World Irish Dancing Championships, and thousands of people had descended on the city from all over the world.

'We're absolutely packed out.' he said. 'But let me see what I can do. There's another party coming in soon and there might have been some cancellations, but I'll need to wait and check. There's other hostels around, but they're pretty full, so we'll find you a couch or something if you're really stuck.'

While the hostel man checked his bookings, I took the opportunity to go for a wander. The area around the hostel was the old industrial heart of the city, where linen among other things had been produced. In fact, Belfast had a major industrial heritage, with factories and shipyards employing thousands in the past. The fateful Titanic had even been built here. However, since the decline of heavy industry, the rise of the terrorist conflict (euphemistically called 'the Troubles') had made it difficult to attract new businesses and industries.

I walked down a dimly-lit street, between two vast red brick factories, tightening my coat against the encroaching night. A small sign indicated a pub on the corner, but its welcome consisted of a bare lightbulb above the door, metal grills on the blacked-out windows, and a buzzer on the entrance. A police Land Rover drove by, reinforced with armoured bodywork like the ones I had seen masked youths throw bottles at on the news.

This may have still been the UK, but it felt quite unfamiliar.

I got back to the hostel, and fortunately the man at the desk had found me a bed thanks to a cancellation. I followed his directions to the dorm, threw my stuff on my bed, and after a quick wash and change, headed off into the city centre to meet Mhairi and her friends.

I was meeting them in a club called Limelight – a place that if tonight was anything to go by, was a young and energetic place that specialised in loud heavy rock music. Now I'm much more of a pub man than a club man – I hate not being able to hear what other people are saying, I like my music to set the atmosphere not dominate it, and I hate not being able to have a seat. So after meeting Mhairi, getting introduced to her friends, spotting a couple of mullets in the crowd (young, trendy ones – the worst kind), and drinking a couple of pints of Guinness, I decided I'd had enough.

Maybe I was being a bit of an antisocial grump, but it had been a long day – over six hours on the train and then a couple on the ferry – and I'd had an early start. I needed my bed. Besides, I wasn't in Ireland to dance the night away in Belfast nightclubs. I was here to hunt mullets.

I'd decided to do a couple of nights in Belfast before heading to Dublin. By happy coincidence, Mel, the American girl I'd met in Inverness and who had told me about the film Mulletville, was aiming to be in Dublin. She'd told me she was doing a college term abroad in Belgium, and was aiming to come over to meet a group of her classmates who were doing a term in Dublin.

Even better, she said she fancied coming on the pilgrimage to Belmullet with me when I told her about it in an email, so to fit in with the flight she'd booked I was going to do two nights in Belfast, then two in Dublin. It would be just enough to see both cities before going west for the real reason for the journey.

It was hard to think of what there was to see in Belfast. This was 2004, shortly before full peace had been achieved. While the worst of the Troubles were clearly over, the city's reputation was still defined, to me at least, by the violence, tension and hot-headed politicians I saw on the news. What jumped out of my guidebook to me as the most compelling tourist attractions, if you could call them that, were the Falls Road and Shankhill Road.

In the west of the city, a major flashpoint for the sectarian violence and terrorism had arisen between these two streets – one Protestant, one Roman Catholic – separated by an ironically-

named 'Peace Wall'. I decided that might be an interesting
place to start, and besides it wasn't very far from my hostel. So
after a leisurely morning, I headed off.

From the main road, the two streets seemed innocuous
enough. Most roads around me were busy, and as I stood
with the old factories behind me I could see all the usual
roadsigns, billboards, adverts, buses and traffic you would
expect to see anywhere else in the UK. On closer inspection,
though, these two particular roads were anything other than
innocuous.

I started with the mainly Protestant Shankhill Road. Huge
murals on walls and gable ends greeted me.

'For God and Ulster', one slogan read. '90 Years of Resistance', said another with a stark image of a signpost pointing
to 'United Kingdom' and 'Peace' in one direction, and to 'Eire'
and 'War' in the other. No compromise here, it seemed.

I walked up the street as far as I felt comfortable. The street
was pretty deserted – it was mid-morning on a weekday – and
in a sense it was like any other street, with shops, pubs, and
terraced houses. But there was a run-down feel about the
place, doubtless evidence of a poverty which fuelled the
bitterness and resentment. There was a definite edge – a
tension, a hard to define feeling that I wasn't entirely welcome.
Granted, the murals were pretty well known as being part of
Belfast's tourism, and most of the few other people I saw out
and about were tourists too, snapping away at the paintings
which were huge and intimidating, but struck me nevertheless
as clearly the result of much time and talent.

The murals here spoke of no compromise, of resistance, even
of fear. This was a community which felt betrayed by the
Union it was loyal to, which feared its neighbours, and feared
the future.

Things were different on the Falls Road, the mainly nationalist, Roman Catholic street which was just over the wall but
obviously a long walk round to get to. There wasn't exactly a
carnival atmosphere, but there was clearly an ambition to

project a message outwards to the wider world. The graffiti and murals spoke of justice (or a lack thereof), of civil liberties, of solidarity with various causes throughout the world that the community felt affinity to, such as those of the Palestinians or Basques.

Yet there was a tension here too. Much venom was directed towards the police and army, whose presence was very much felt, due to a huge fortified watchtower which dominated the Falls Road. The walls spoke of oppression. One mural, sitting in between a message of solidarity with the military campaign in the Basque country on the one side and a condemnation of police brutality on the other, expressed outrage at rubber bullets.

It explained that the Royal Ulster Constabulary, the police force which had been long-hated by the Nationalist and Republican communities, was introducing a supposedly deadly new form of rubber bullet. To emphasise the point, the mural depicted a silhouetted line of children at the bottom, ostensibly to represent those children from their community who had died from such ammunition. However, only three black outlines of children were painted on the left of the wall, the gap across the rest of the wall suggesting there was room for at least another dozen fatalities.

A morbid side of me couldn't help wondering if there was a mural artist somewhere near the Falls Road who was secretly frustrated that not enough children had yet died in his community to fill the line and make the political point.

I explored other parts of the city, too. The vibrant city centre, boasting all the usual high street names, had shops whose heavy shutters swung down at 5 o'clock and turned the retail area into a ghost town. There was the beautiful City Hall, the Union Jack flying high above it, no doubt to the consternation of one half of the city. And the riverside was impressive, with clear evidence of regeneration consisting of modern civic buildings, luxury flats, and the two giant cranes which stood at the harbour as a testament to the shipbuilding industry that so dominated the city in the past.

I also took a wander through the beautiful Victorian-era campus of Queen's University, and over the river to East Belfast, where the red, white and blue flags and murals shouted out the siege mentality of another Loyalist community.

After a hard day's touristing, I retreated to the hostel. I got talking to two of my dorm-mates, an American and a Canadian, who separately were travelling throughout Europe. Although I'd enjoyed Belfast so far, it had been a bit lonely. Although I'd been out unexpectedly with Mhairi and her friends the previous night, the conversation hadn't exactly been easy in the club, and my day of exploring hadn't led me to meet anyone else. Such is the peril of solo travelling.

I dragged my two fellow tourists out for a couple of pints. Very much following our noses in a city none of us knew, we stumbled fortuitously upon a textbook Irish pub. Dark, smoky interior, not much on tap beyond Guinness, an impressive array of Irish whiskeys behind the bar, road signs speaking of distances to Irish towns, and a fiddle band thumping out traditional music in the corner. It was so much the stereo-typical Irish pub that you see in just about any city in the world these days, that it was hard to believe we were actually in Ireland.

After a few Guinnesses over the usual travellers' tales that young backpackers tend to bore each other with, we headed back to the hostel. I slept soundly, and headed off early the next morning for Dublin.

I've always preferred trains to buses, for a number of reasons. For a start, I'm just over six feet tall, which makes it hard for me to stretch out on buses. I also get very sick if I read on the road, whereas if I am on the train, motion is smoother and it's one more thing I can do to pass the time. I ended up taking the bus to Dublin, however, because it was much cheaper and easier to figure out.

Tolerating the lack of leg room, I enjoyed the journey as we passed out of Belfast and into the Northern Irish countryside, the Union Jacks and red, white and blue curb stones, or Irish tricolours and political posters, telling us whose territory we were going through. I wondered how much of this province was segregated, how many areas insisted on declaring their identity (which I felt was as much about who they weren't as who they were) above getting on with their lives. I tried not to judge, mock or condemn – it was too easy to make jokes about the pettiness and the angry politicians who appeared to folk on my side of the Irish Sea as parodies of themselves, since I'd not myself lived through those thirty years and more of violence.

At least the political propaganda served a purpose though, in that its sudden absence indicated the border with the Republic of Ireland, wordlessly doing the job of a customs point or road sign.

I arrived at the bus station in Dublin and immediately got lost. By mistaking the 'bus' icon on my map for the bus station, rather than the bus company's main city centre ticket outlet as it actually was, my backpack and I ended up taking a very long walkabout through the streets of the city, dodging road works, shoppers, office-workers and absolute legions of tourists. This was a busy place. Thankfully, though, I eventually found my hostel – a small place in the Temple Bar district of the city.

Temple Bar was one of the main hubs for Dublin's ever-growing nightlife, popularised by budget airlines enabling hoards of hen and stag nights from across the water in Britain to come piling over to get wasted in the name of a good time. It was noisy, chaotic, but also quaint and friendly in its own way. I hadn't really chosen the hostel or area, as Mel had booked in for the following night when she would arrive from Belgium and I felt it would be nice to be in the same place – but I would put up with it. The hostel, as far as I could discern from the staff, was owned by a Chinese family, and an angry sign at reception written in poor English told me to watch out for the curfew, after which time I would not get back in at night.

I had a quick look around the empty dorm I was booked into, which seemed sufficiently clean and functional, dumped my rucksack, and headed off for an explore.

The river Liffy separated Temple Bar from the city centre, and so I took a stroll along the riverside. The buildings along the front seemed pleasant – a mix of bland modern architecture and ornate, grand Victorian construction. I headed into the city centre, but it was hard to find anything of interest as most of the city appeared to be getting dug up by road workers (I wondered if, in an ironic twist, the labourers were all English), and the crowds were overwhelming. I wondered why Dublin was so busy, and then I realised it was nothing out of the ordinary. This was the capital of one of the most popular countries in the world, a place of mystery, myth, romance and leprechauns, which attracted Americans, Asians and Europeans in their thousands every year. The tourist economy had clearly helped Dublin boom into a thriving city.

It didn't especially grab me, though. It just didn't feel very . . . Irish. Sure the people spoke in Irish accents – most of them anyway – but the shops, buildings, restaurants and so on all suggested this was a fairly standard, growing, small European capital city. The brand names, the efficient-looking public transport, even the euro to which Ireland had recently converted, all made Dublin look and feel not particularly Irish. And just had I had found in Belfast, Dublin's own examples of the nation's most irritating export, the Irish pub, didn't necessarily mean that I was in Ireland.

That night, I met up with a guy named Kev, a friend of friends. They'd insisted I should look him up and that I would get on with him. I was glad of the chance for company, and so after making contact Kev and I agreed to go for a couple of pints that evening in a bar just across the road from my hostel.

Kev was an absolutely lovely guy and we did indeed get on well. A trainee solicitor, he was a tall, well-built chap with a bright, cheeky smile and an infectious laugh. We got on brilliantly, and he loved the reason for my trip when I explained it. I told him all about my Albanian trip, my experiences of Ireland so far, and the little I knew about Belmullet, which disconcertingly he had never heard of.

Guinness was the order of the evening. Although I tended to prefer heavy ales to lagers, I wasn't a huge fan of Guinness, and had drunk it in Northern Ireland simply because the pubs didn't really boast much else. Here in Dublin, other dark beers were even harder to find. Thankfully though, it tasted a lot smoother than it had in Belfast or indeed anywhere in Scotland, and I took quite a liking to it.

Another major difference in the pub culture was the clean air. Ireland had introduced its controversial ban on smoking in public places just a couple of weeks previously, and it was quite literally a breath of fresh air. I've never been a smoker and generally detest the smell of it and how, without even having a puff yourself, you could still come home from a night in the pub with your clothes and hair smelling like the back end of a horse.

That said, I had been a little dubious about whether the ban would work. All the stereotypical images of the Irish pub were of dark, fusty old hovels where the smoke added atmosphere, and where old men had sat on the same stool smoking the same tobacco for years. I reckoned there would be huge resistance, and it would sap much of the feel of the traditional pub.

To the contrary, though, it felt great – pubs were brighter, airier, more welcoming, and more pleasant to be in without the smoke, and it was having seen it work in Ireland that led me to so keenly support the ban's introduction in Scotland a couple of years later.

One advantage of the smoke, however, had been that it masked other unpleasant smells. After a few pints, Kev took me to a nightclub round the corner, where for the first time I experienced a club that smelt not of cigarette smoke but of its true aroma – stale and spilt alcohol and obnoxious body odour. It was an improvement, but certainly not by much.

By the end of the night, however, I was past caring. When I realised my hostel's curfew was impending, I bade a hasty farewell to Kev, who wished me well in the mullet-hunting, and off I sped. I missed the curfew, hammered on the hostel door, got let in by a sullen-looking staff member, and collapsed in my bed. Tired, Guinnessed-out, and a step closer to Belmullet.

I was awoken earlier than I really wanted by my mobile phone going off. Bleary-eyed, I rolled over, picked it up and saw it was an international number I did not recognise. I answered.

It was Mel. There had been a strike by Belgian railway workers, which meant she couldn't get to the airport as quickly as she'd hoped, and she'd missed her flight. It being with a cheap budget airline, there was no potential to reschedule. Her long weekend in Ireland wouldn't be possible.

That was a real shame. I was really looking forward to seeing her again after meeting her in Inverness, and to some company on the forthcoming journey to Belmullet. She'd shown such enthusiasm for my mullet mission, had dug up 'Mulletville' for me, and was keen to come to help me bag my next goal. As it was, I'd just have to press on alone.

Mel did, however, tell me to go and meet her friends who were studying in Dublin. She'd been in touch with them, and said they were all meeting later that afternoon in front of the central Post Office, and would be looking out for me.

So after a couple of hours' more sleep and a bit of idle touristing, I headed off to meet them. I was quite keen to see the Post Office – it had been the site of the last stand of the Irish Republicans during the Easter Rising in 1916, the rebellion that eventually led to the partition of Ireland into Northern Ireland, which was retained by the UK, and the Irish Free State, which later become the Republic of Ireland. The Post Office had been pretty much demolished, and I turned up early to have a look around.

It had been rebuilt, and the interior was adorned with huge paintings that depicted the destruction of its previous incarnation. It was one of the few icons of the Irish independence movement that I'd seen in the city. Most of the things in Dublin that emphasised its unique character were either on the tacky side – cuddly leprechauns in the windows of shops – or the modern, future-orientated side, such as the iconic Needle, which towered above the city centre. There was very little that dwelt on Ireland's tragic and painful history. This was a sign of real confidence in its identity – an identity that was positive and outward-looking, unlike what I felt to be the reactionary identities north of the border.

I met Mel's half-dozen or so friends outside the Post Office. I spotted them very easily, as they were all a certain caricature of American college kids, and very like Mel: hair that shouted rebellion, Che Guevara t-shirts, exuberant voices, and names like Zane or Mary-Lou. Although I had got on well with Mel, I found her friends a bit of a handful once we adjourned to a pub. They had loud laughs and a puerile sense of humour, and although I was only twenty-five myself, they were still in their late teens and made me feel very old indeed. I didn't hang around long before making my excuses.

I had nowhere particular to be, I just wanted to be on my own for a bit. Yet I was getting a bit bored with travelling by myself and had been looking forward to Mel's company partly so I'd have someone to talk to on the trip. But I wasn't feeling quite myself after last night's late finish, and Dublin wasn't really grabbing me.

I spent the rest of the day just footering about – exploring a few streets, buying a few postcards, checking the bus times for the next day, and getting something to eat in a cheap and cheerful takeaway joint – before getting an early night.

'Eh, can I get a single to Ballina please', I said, stressing the town's name to make it rhyme with 'marina'.

'Ballin*aaaa*', shot back the bored-looking girl behind the

desk at the bus station, adding more 'a's to the end of the word than seemed necessary.

'Sorry,' I said, emphasising my Scottish accent to see if it would warm her tone and elicit some Celtic comradeship. It didn't.

Ballina, or Ballin*aaaa* if you like, was a town over in the west of Ireland, where I was due to change before heading further west towards the very edge of the country, to the Mullet Peninsula, and the village of Belmullet. My destination. My second mullet.

It was a quiet bus and the journey was punctuated by stops in pretty villages and towns along the way. In most, the buildings were painted in bright colours, flowers adorned the outside of shops and pubs, and there seemed a real buzz about small-town Ireland. Which was all very welcome, because the scenery was awful.

It reminded me of Belgium, in a way. A country I love, Belgium boasts some of the dullest landscape I've ever seen, but more than makes up for it with beautifully ornate, extravagant and ostentatious urban architecture. The towns and cities are well-kempt, attractive and brimming with history.

It was something of a contrast to Scotland, where our scenery is among the best you could find in Europe, and our small towns are all-too-frequently complete shitholes that never recovered from the decline in heavy industry, or were faded coastal towns that lost out some decades ago to Mediterranean resorts in the fight for Scottish tourists.

I guess I was spoilt, living in the Highlands of Scotland, generally regarded as one of the most beautiful parts of the world. Scottish people might stereotypically be seen as a bit dourer and less charismatic than their cousins across the water in Ireland, but I sensed there was certainly a whole heap more to look at in Scotland than here. The scenery seemed drab – boggy, barren, windswept, and uninspiring. No wonder the Irish, like the Belgians, had put some impressive effort into making their towns look great.

Apart from Ballina. There wasn't much to it, I discovered in the couple of hours' break between buses, other than some tired-looking buildings that badly needed a lick of paint, and a couple of bog standard pubs, in one of which I imbibed some admittedly excellent food and a refreshing pint of Guinness.

While there, I caught sight of a newspaper on my table and – for something to do along with my lunch – I browsed through it. It was a local rag, all exhortation from local councillors and tedious coverage of school prize-givings. I always felt a bit sorry for local papers often having to plunge the depths of mundanity in order to fill a few column inches. When growing up, for instance, one of our local papers, the Stornoway Gazette, would give far too much space each week to a local columnist's ramblings about the previous seven days' weather in North Uist.

The paper I was reading was a particularly uninspiring example of local news, so much so that I couldn't help thinking that my visit to Belmullet was probably among the more exciting things this corner of County Mayo had seen for some time.

In that case, the thought occurred, why hadn't I considered approaching them with my story? They could perhaps have helped me find out a little about the place and helped me make some contacts. Of course they might – perhaps rightly – have ranked it as less worthy than local planning decisions or school prize-givings, but nevertheless I stored the idea away at the back of my mind.

Before long, I was on the bus to Belmullet. This time it was busier, and I found myself sitting next to a man, perhaps in his thirties, who insisted on talking to me all the way. I learned that he came from Blacksod, an unappealing-sounding place that was beyond Belmullet at the far end of the Mullet Peninsula. He was a keen Liverpool fan, told me all about his family, and was a panel-beater by trade. In a part of the world as sparsely-populated as the view out of the window suggested, I was unconvinced that there would really be enough panels for him to beat.

He asked what my impressions of Ireland had been so far. I told him I'd enjoyed it, in a tone I felt was minimal without being rude. To be honest, I was more keen on enjoying my own space and listening to music on my headphones, but my new friend didn't seem to sense this. He asked what I thought of the beer.

'Alright, but I like dark beers, and there only seems to be Guinness.'

'Ah you should try Smithwicks,' he said. 'Lovely stuff.' We were pulling into Belmullet, where I could leave my travelling companion. 'Go there,' he said pointing out a pub on the main street we were driving down. 'MacDonell's, it's really nice, it's always crowded. And you can get Smithwicks there.'

With that useful gem of information, I breathed a sigh of relief as I got off the bus and headed for the main hotel in the village, which seemed from my Lonely Planet guide book to be a decent and welcoming enough place.

'You can only stay a night,' barked the stern-looking woman who met me at reception, which consisted of a small table in the dimly-lit hallway.

'Oh, are you fully-booked?' I enquired.

'We're closed tomorrow – it's Good Friday. Everywhere'll be closed.'

Bugger. Of course. This was Easter, in very rural, very Roman Catholic Ireland. Not the best of planning on my part. Not content with trying to stay in Belfast when thousands of Irish dancers from across the globe were in town, I was now attempting to find a bed in a small village on the Easter weekend when everyone would be spending time with their families and having back to back masses.

'There's one or two bed and breakfasts you might get into for tomorrow,' said the woman, 'but I doubt it. I'll get you some phone numbers anyway.'

After I had enjoyed my warm welcome to this homely establishment, I dropped off my bag in my room, and went to have a look round Belmullet.

It was a small village, at a guess no more than a couple of thousand people, and consisted of a few streets converging on a roundabout that appeared to constitute the centre of town. There was the usual range of shops – a post office, grocer's, hardware shop, a couple of pubs, that sort of thing – but not that many people around. It was late on in the afternoon, and starting to get dark. I decided to explore the village after a night's rest, when hopefully I would be in better spirits.

Later though, after phoning a number given to me by the hotel and finding myself a B&B just up the road for the following night, I decided to go out and explore the pubs. I walked right past McDonell's, recommended by the panel-beater on the bus, which didn't in fact look all that appealing from the outside. Instead, I crossed the road and entered The Anchor.

The Anchor looked neat and olde-worlde from the outside, but it was pretty dead inside. There were no more than three or four groups of people in that night, in what was a pretty spacious pub. The interior was dark, with wooden panelling, dark tables and leather seats. Some football was on the television – a European match featuring Celtic, on which the volume was down and to which nobody seemed to be paying much attention.

I claimed a seat at the bar, and ordered a pint of Guinness. I looked around. No ubiquitous drunk propping up the bar and engaging me in incomprehensible banter. A barmaid who was efficient but not chatty. No energetic band in the corner. Not much atmosphere. Not much craic, as they call it. I browsed idly through my phone, refraining from sending any messages due to the higher cost of texting from a foreign network.

While I wondered how long I could get away with sitting sipping my beer and re-reading old text messages before people started noticing me as a Johnny No Mates, a burly man with a moustache came up to the bar next to me.

'Two Guinnesses, please, hen,' he declared loudly to the woman behind the bar. He was unmistakeably Glaswegian.

'There's an accent I didn't expect to hear,' I chipped in.

'Aye,' said the man with a note of surprise. 'And waur you from yersel'?'

'Inverness,' I replied.

'And whit are you doin' here?'

'Just on holiday,' I said, not keen yet to divulge the reason for my mission.

'Well come over and join us – you'll have a pint?'

'We're engineers,' explained John, my new acquaintance. His co-worker and co-drinker, Peter, was from Downpatrick in Northern Ireland. 'They've discovered gas offshore from here, and we're building a pipeline. There's going to be a lot of money coming into Belmullet in the next few years – it's a booming place.'

I'd not seen any evidence of an economic powerhouse in the making in my first few hours, but I would take John's word for it.

'So how come you're here? Why choose this place for a holiday?' John, the chattier of the two, quizzed me. I took a deep breath and decided to tell the truth.

'I'm trying to visit every place in the world that has the word 'mullet' in its name. This is my second.'

'Aye?' said John, his look of surprise slightly muted, suggesting he didn't quite believe me. 'Where have you been so far?'

'Just here and Albania. And there's Australia, the Caribbean, the USA and Canada to go still.'

'And what do you do when you get to the places?'

I paused. John had stumped me. I wasn't really sure. What did I do? What had I done in Albania? Not much, apart from photograph the road sign and drive on. And what was there to do in Belmullet? Equally not much, except sit back a few years and wait for the gas pipeline to be completed. I wondered if they'd throw a big gas pipeline party.

'Well . . .' I struggled to think of something. 'Not a lot really, just tick it off the list and move on. But I guess I'll explore a bit and enjoy myself while I'm here. It's only a couple of nights, anyway.'

'Good luck,' said Peter. 'There's really not a lot to do here. It's a bit of a shithole to be honest. We spend most of our spare time here.'

That filled me with hope.

After a couple more drinks, the engineers left as they had an early start at work the next morning, and I decided to head to bed too. After all, I had a hard day's doing 'not a lot' in 'a bit of a shithole' to look forward to.

SIX

A One Bus Stop Mullet

The next morning, after breakfast, I checked out of the hotel and walked across the roundabout and along the road to the bed and breakfast I'd lined up. It was a little out of the centre of the village (still only ten minutes' walk or so) and overlooked the bay round which the beginnings of the Mullet Peninsula huddled. The peninsula was low-lying, bleak, and the bay itself just a shore of rock and seaweed. The landscape was too flat for a further horizon. There was just the land, the sea and the sky. Nothing else. Not even evidence of the lighthouses implied in the poem by Donald S Murray, the poem that had led me to come to this small village.

The guest house was immaculate and my room was lovely, but the owner, a dreary and uninterested woman, barely spoke to me as she gave me my key. I wondered whether she had been looking forward to having Good Friday off before I'd called.

Here I was, I thought, as I walked back into the village centre with the aim of seeing what there was to do. Belmullet. On the Mullet Peninsula. I didn't feel like Neil Armstrong setting foot on the moon, I didn't feel like Christopher Columbus as he became the first European to discover America. Apart from all those poor Vikings we always seem to conveniently forget about.

Mind you, I've no idea exactly what Armstrong or Columbus actually felt, but surely there must have been some sense of thrill, of excitement, of creating history. No doubt, too, a considerable fear of the unknown, of how the trip would end, of how the natives would react (although granted, that was probably less of a fear for Neil Armstrong).

I, on the other hand, making a giant leap for mulletology, felt . . . underwhelmed. Like I was spending a quiet day in a small village on the edge of Ireland, and nothing more. I sighed, and decided to throw myself into Belmullet to see what there was to discover.

I walked down to the roundabout in the centre of the village, went over it, passing just down from the hotel that was so fervently observing Good Friday, and followed the road that went off in the opposite direction. Up the hill on the right I could see what looked like a school. On the left, some sort of agricultural warehouse.

Then nothing. No mullets. No lighthouses. Nothing.

The village just stopped. Nothing to mark the boundary except a roadsign about a hundred metres further out at a junction in the road, directing drivers into Belmullet. Nothing beyond it, other than flat, boggy moorland and a grey sky above. I took a photo of the roadsign, for posterity.

I walked back, and popped into the post office. Thankfully, they sold Belmullet postcards. I bought a handful – some to send home, a couple to keep as proof I'd been here, and one to send to Mel. If Belgian train drivers had stopped her being here, at least I could send her a souvenir.

Then, out of the corner of my eye on one of the shelves, I noticed a book. 'Within The Mullet', by Rita Nolan. I picked it up. It was a history of the Mullet Peninsula, or 'The Mullet' as it was known. I flicked through it.

> 'For my sister May,
> who loved the Mullet'

. . . said the dedication inside. I wondered what personal best May had achieved in her mullet-spotting scores.

I read on a bit. It seemed to be a pretty comprehensive

history, from prehistoric times to the modern era, and while it wasn't cheap at 16 euro, I decided to buy it. A book entitled 'Within the Mullet' was too good to miss out on.

Fast running out of things to do, I then went for a walk around the bay. On my way, my eye was caught by a sign declaring 'Birds of the Mullet'. I went over to investigate. Such was my obsession with mullets these days that the word 'mullet' would often jump out at me if I saw it. So much so that I still to this day find it hard walking past Millet's, the outdoor store, on Inverness high street without checking that it isn't actually 'Mullet's'.

'Dramatic scenery, wildlife and a variety of bird species make the Mullet a year-round attraction for anyone interested in our natural heritage and especially interesting for bird-watchers.' Gripping stuff I thought, as I read the interpretation. Although I did dispute the validity of 'dramatic'. 'Sand dunes and coastal *machair* grasslands are plentiful and there are extensive wetlands associated with lakes such as Termon-carragh and Cross Lough . . .' I'll spare you the rest of the excitement.

Moving on past the sign and over a bridge across a canal (which technically separated the peninsula from the mainland), I meandered round the bay. Other than a view back to the village from a distance, it didn't render much, although it was a pleasant enough stroll.

Just beyond the bay was the road which headed down the peninsula to Blacksod. I had thought about walking down – it would have taken me perhaps a couple of hours, in the absence of buses – but decided I couldn't be bothered. Besides, I wasn't too sure what there was to do down there, except get my panel beaten by the guy I met on the bus.

He was probably taking Good Friday off, anyway.

With nothing better to do, I went back to the B&B, lay down on the bed, put my headphones in my ears, and put some music on while I had another flick through 'Within the Mullet'.

'*We have waited long for a history of the Mullet Peninsula, but the wait has been worthwhile,*' enthused Father Kevin Hegarty, presumably the local priest, who had penned the foreword. I turned over to chapter one, which included an explanation of the name Belmullet.

'*There is some controversy about how the Mullet got its name,*' the author wrote. '*Many people believe it is called after the fish of that name because of its rather similar shape, and so Caesar Otway was told by local people when he visited the area in the 1830s. It is more generally believed, however, that the name originated in the Irish word* 'Muileat', *meaning diamond, because the peninsula is indeed roughly of an elongated diamond shape. Later, the Irish name became corrupted to* 'Béal an Mhuirthead', *though among native Irish speakers* 'Béal 'Mhuileat' *is still sometimes heard. Whatever its origin may be, such a mundane name gives no inkling of the extraordinary beauty of the place.*'

Good grief, she enjoyed getting carried away. Extraordinary beauty? That was pushing it a bit, I felt. But then if you're writing a history of a place, I guess you have to big it up. If the writer had been a bit more realistic about the scenery, after all, Father Hegarty might not have been quite so complimentary in his foreword. And then where would we have been?

So there we go, I thought. Nothing to do with fish, nothing to do with the haircut. Just a quirk of language – Belmullet was an Anglicised corruption of Béal an Mhuirthead, which was itself a corruption of the Irish word for 'diamond'. Just like Mullet in Albania, a coincidence of language. What was I doing here in this strange, quiet village? Not discovering anything about the nature of the haircut, that was for sure. I was following a whim, and not really feeling much more enlightened as a result.

After a bit of a snooze, brought on no doubt by the excitement of 'Within the Mullet', I headed into the village centre and got a burger at a lifeless café in which just a handful of others were sitting. It was now dark. I went for a stroll up the hill past the two pubs and along the road I had originally come in by bus. There I found a sign standing bold in the darkness:

ÚDARÁS
NA
GAELTACHTA

– – – – – –

Béal
an
Mhuirthead

'Route of the Gaeltacht', I guessed. At least, I knew what Gaeltacht was – the land of the Gael or Gaelic speaker – equivalent to the Gaidhealtachd in Scotland, and presumably pronounced much the same. Scots Gaelic had a lot of similarities with Irish Gaelic. Údarás, I surmised, was perhaps something like route or tour, only because of the squiggly arrow logo next to it, which suggested some sort of Gaelic language trail for tourists to follow.

Belmullet, and County Mayo generally, was apparently one of the few places left in Ireland where Irish, or Irish Gaelic, was still spoken as a first lanaguage. I'd not heard a word of it, mind you, since arriving.

Not that I would have understood it. Although I was born in the Highlands and grew up in the Western Isles, very much a Gaelic-speaking area, my parents were from England and I learned only a little in school. Moreover, had I heard Irish Gaelic it would have been too fast to pick out anything more than the occasional familiar sound or word. Scots Gaelic, while much the same in structure, takes an awful lot more time (not to mention a lot more letters) to say what is needed to be said.

Like most languages, I suppose, it mirrors the culture and the people. The story is told of a Spaniard who visits a Gaelic-speaking area of Scotland and explains the Spanish concept of 'mañana' to a local. He says it means 'tomorrow' and is used in Spain to nonchalantly and non-committally put a task off perhaps until tomorrow, another day, some undefined time in the future. He asks his new friend if he understands.

'Yes,' replies the Gaelic speaker, thoughtfully. 'We have a word a little similar to that in Gaelic, but it doesn't quite convey the same sense of urgency.'

I decided to round the night off with a pint. I went to the Anchor, where I had been the previous night. No sign of the gas engineers, or any other patrons for that matter. Where was everyone? It was Good Friday, granted, but still nevertheless a Friday. Did communities like this close down totally on such days? I didn't for a second believe that religion still had such a strong grip that nobody dared go out. As I sat nursing a pint of Guinness, though, that's exactly how it seemed.

After I'd finished my pint, I crossed the road to McDonell's, the pub the panel-beater had recommended to me, to see if there was any more life there. It was considerably smaller – a bar running down the left hand side, seats on the right, and not much else. It was a lot barer and more soulless than the Anchor. There were a few people in, who all looked up at me for a second, before going back to their drinks or conversations. Had there been a pianist, I am sure he'd have stopped playing for a brief moment.

I ordered a pint of Smithwicks, remembering the panel-beater's endorsement of it, and sat down at a table which for some reason had a huge pile of the local paper, the same one I'd read in the pub in Ballina. I re-read it, uninterested, and once my pint had settled, I took a sip. It was foul. I drank it as quickly as I could bear, and headed off to bed.

There was only one bus out of the village the next morning, Saturday, and I needed to catch it. I had one more night left in Ireland, and my plan was to spend it in Derry, Northern

Ireland's second city, before heading to catch the ferry from Belfast on Sunday morning and getting home sometime late that night – ready to go back to work the following day.

My bus was to Ballina, from where I would catch another bus to Sligo, and change there for Derry. I arrived early at Belmullet's one bus stop. Not only was I keen to ensure that I was in time for my bus, I was also pretty keen to get out of town. The woman in the B&B had typified my experience of Belmullet – she'd served an admittedly fantastic breakfast which would keep me stocked up for most of the day, but she barely spoke to me, asked nothing about the reason for my visit, said nothing like 'welcome to Belmullet', and had generally made me feel like something of an inconvenience.

And that's what I'd felt about the place as a whole – nobody else had really spoken to me, and while admittedly I'd not exactly made an effort to stop strangers on the street to engage them in conversation, I'd still not experienced the supposedly 'traditional' Irish welcome. The gas engineers, both from other parts of the world, had been the people I'd spoken to most.

Not that I really blamed Belmullet – it wasn't really a bustling tourist destination. Why should I have been treated any differently? It had been my choice to come to a small rural village in the middle of the Easter weekend, after all.

My thoughts were distracted by the arrival of the bus. I was the only person waiting.

'Ballina?' asked the bus driver, a portly gentleman with a small moustache, a round face and a cheerful smile. I replied in the affirmative.

'Fling your bag underneath,' he said breezily, opening the boot, 'and hop on!'

I sat on the front row of the bus, just behind and to the left of the driver. As I was the only passenger he had started to engage me in conversation as we waited.

'So, you just visiting then?'

'Yes, I'm from Inverness in Scotland. Just on a week's holiday round Ireland.'

'What on earth brings you to Belmullet, then?'

'I'm visiting every place in the world that's got the word "mullet" in its name,' I replied, matter-of-factly.

The bus driver's face lit up with a mix of fascination and disbelief and he burst out laughing – a big hearty, belly laugh.

'No way! Really?'

'Yup,' I replied, not sure what else to add.

'Every place in the world with "mullet" . . . good grief. Seriously? Why? Where have you been?'

I began telling him a little more about my trip to Albania, how I'd found reference to Belmullet in an old teacher's book of poetry, and about the other mullets I was hoping to visit. He laughed. I told him how it had all started with the travels round Eastern Europe with Niall. He laughed again, listening to my story intently, punctuating it with an occasional 'no way?' or 'you never did!' or 'that's fantastic!'

'Well, I think that's a brilliant idea, I really do,' he declared when I'd finished. 'It's grand that you came out here – good luck with the rest of the journey!'

Our conversation dried up as an elderly woman got on just as we were about to leave. But he left me with a big smile on my face, as I sat back and took in the bleak County Mayo countryside.

The first person in Belmullet to show any interest in the trip, the one person to appreciate it just for what it was – a madcap, pointless adventure – was the bus driver on the way out of town. His laughter and his endorsement of my admittedly eccentric efforts made me feel it hadn't been wasted after all. I wasn't doing this for any higher purpose, I wasn't even doing it to find out more about the hair cut to be honest – I was just doing it because I could, and because it was fun; and he loved the idea.

My mood brightened, and I began feeling a lot more content with myself for having attempted the mission and made it out to the remote west coast of Ireland – all thanks to the bus driver.

*

I arrived in Derry having learned my lesson on the accom-modation front. After landing in Belfast in the middle of an international dancing competition, and in Belmullet just as hatches were being battened down for Easter, I decided I wouldn't run another risk in Derry, and phoned ahead to a hostel I plucked out of the guide book. As if to justify my forward-planning, they'd just had a huge booking made for that night and there were only a couple of free beds remaining. Phew.

An attractive wee place, Derry was built around an old walled town, one of the oldest still-complete city walls in Europe. You could walk around the walls and get some fine views – the city was set in the midst of beautiful countryside, and had a huge river, the Foyle, running through it. It was a nice end to the trip and I really enjoyed exploring it.

It was no idyll, though. As Northern Ireland's second city it had seen more than its fair share of 'the Troubles'. Its name, even, was something of a bone of contention – Derry was a widely popular name, particularly among Republicans, but the Loyalist population called it Londonderry. Rather than taking sides on this debate, the local BBC radio station was called Radio Foyle. Apparently, local media would often refer to 'Derry/Londonderry', giving it the nickname 'Stroke city'.

One area, known as the Derry Free State, had been the scene of one of the most controversial moments in The Troubles, when thirteen nationalist civil rights protesters were shot dead by soldiers in the 1960s. Since then there has been claim and counter-claim about whether it was military brutality or whether there had been shots fired first by Republican terror-ists. It's probably one of those sad occasions when nobody will ever know the real truth.

The inevitable murals on buildings in the Derry Free State, clearly visible from the city walls, portrayed some of the iconic images from that day. I went for a walk through those streets, and was struck by one slogan – 'Our revenge will be the laughter of our children.' What better mantra for politics in

Northern Ireland could there be, I thought: that people should put aside violence and claim a victory only if their children were happy.

Meanwhile round the other side of the walls, overlooking a loyalist housing estate, I could see a gable end slogan which blared:

'Londonderry West Bank Loyalists still under siege. No surrender!'

Clearly the tensions were still a long way from being resolved.

In fact, as I explored Derry more that day, I couldn't help thinking it reminded me a little of Jerusalem. Niall and I had spent around five days there on our travels together, as we'd moved south through Eastern Europe and into the Middle East. Jerusalem, like Derry, was built on a hill around a historic walled city. A city which, like Derry, was claimed by two sides. A small, compact boiling pot, which served only to exaggerate and emphasise the tensions, divisions and difficulties.

Jerusalem was not the only other city I'd been to that lay on a faith-based faultline. In fact, over the years I'd notched up quite a tally of cities that were known for their religious divisions.

Pristina. Mitrovica. Mostar. Sarajevo.

Glasgow.

None of them, apart from Jerusalem however, saw the tension seemingly embodied by a single, highly visible structure in which so much history was locked. As I walked around the walls of the old city in Derry, looking out across rolling hillsides where communities stared across at each other like medieval armies, it could easily, with a small stretch of the imagination, have been Jerusalem.

I liked Derry a lot, though – there was a lovely character to the place despite the division. I had a nice day exploring, and when I caught the bus to Belfast the next morning, it drew my time in Ireland to an end.

It had been fun exploring the neighbours over the water. I knew there was a lot more to Ireland than I'd seen, but I'd managed to pack a lot into my week. Dublin, certainly, had been over-run with tourists, and Belmullet had been something of an underwhelming experience, but it had still been great to see it.

Of course, what mattered most now was that I'd visited my second mullet. It was now two down, five to go.

The mission continued.

Many months later, I quite randomly met an Irish girl in a pub. We got talking, and she said she was from County Mayo.

'Right, I was just in Mayo a while back on holiday,' I said. 'What part?'

'Belmullet, though I live in Galway now.' It was truly a small world, I thought.

'No way, I visited there! I spent two nights in Belmullet!'

'Seriously?' said the girl with some surprise. 'I can only ask . . . why?'

I told her.

She called me a nutcase. But she liked the idea.

'What did everyone there make of it?' She said 'everyone' as if there had been a great civic reception to greet me, and perhaps crowds lining the streets to welcome me to my second mullet. I smiled wryly at the thought, and explained to her that the only person to show any real enthusiasm or appreciation for the mission had been the bus driver on the way out of town.

'Describe him, I might know him,' she insisted.

I told her as much as I could remember about the driver – his appearance, mannerism, accent.

'Paddy Soft Arse!!' she declared.

'Paddy Soft Arse?'

'Yep, that's what we used to call him – he did the school run. Lovely bloke, called Paddy, but he always put a cushion on the driver's seat instead of sitting directly on it, so we called him Paddy Soft Arse.'

I laughed. Such a typically Irish nickname. Well, the one inhabitant of Belmullet who had actually appreciated my mission was now no longer anonymous to me. He'd cheered me up no end after a couple of drab days in the Mullet.

So here's to you, Paddy Soft Arse.

SEVEN

Itchy Feet in Inverness

Two down, five to go.

Ireland hadn't been a rip-roaring adventure that would keep guests captivated at dinner parties, or my grandchildren giggling as I retold stories by an open fire one day in the future. But, I reasoned, it wasn't really supposed to have been. I'd just gone out there, visited a mullet, and come home again. Mission as accomplished as it could have been.

The rest of 2004 went well, not only in terms of the mission progressing, but also in terms of the rest of my life, which hadn't totally been sidelined by mullets. I still had a job to keep me occupied and friends and family to catch up with. Over the year or two since I'd started the mission, I'd slowly and bit by bit told folk I knew about the mission, starting with the friends I judged to have the most off-beat sense of humour and who would be least likely to think me odd. They appreciated hearing how I'd got on in Ireland, and even my parents enjoyed hearing about the mission. I'd wondered, when I first told my mum and dad, what they would make of the silly idea, but thankfully they thought it sounded good fun – or at least, they were too polite and supportive to tell me otherwise.

Meanwhile, Kieran and I had even considered planning another aid convoy, perhaps back to Albania. We booked two weeks off in July, but when the trip fell through at the last minute, we just packed our bags and did a two-week tour of Belgium, the Netherlands, and northern France instead.

I'd been to Belgium before, of course, but the Netherlands was a new country for both Kieran and me to tick off, and we both really liked it. The food and beer were great, the people friendly, and the places we visited, including Amsterdam and The Hague, had great feels to them. It was also the summer of football's 2004 World Cup, and the country was festooned in orange in support of the national team.

Kieran was even moved to buy an orange t-shirt in a shop. It had some writing on and he didn't know what it meant but figured it couldn't be too offensive. We discovered later from a local that in English it meant 'score with me!'

That, sadly, was one of the very few proper, non-mullet based holidays I would have for a number of years, and as I write this, it still is. The fact that I was now committed to the mission meant I had to save up my annual leave – and as much money as I could – so I couldn't do other things with my holidays, like go away with friends, or go to places I actually wanted to visit. For instance, I was keen to go back to the Balkans, or get to the likes of Iceland or New Zealand for the first time, two countries I'd heard nothing but fantastic things about and which were top of my post-mullet travel wish list.

A group of friends from around the country had, for the last couple of years, invited me join them in Cornwall where they rented a large house for two weeks in the summer and spent the time beachcombing, reading, relaxing and hanging around in pubs drinking beer in the sunshine.

It sounded wonderful, but each time I had to tell them that I was saving for my next mullet adventure.

Indeed, I had to consider a major question upon my return from Belmullet – where next for the mission? I'd ticked off the two European mullets, in Albania and Ireland. The ones left over were in Canada, the Caribbean, the USA and Australia. However, those places were a long distance, and a big pile of cash, away from Inverness.

I tended towards Australia, though, for two reasons. The first reason was some lovely people from Brisbane, in the Australian state of Queensland, who stayed with me one summer after contacting me through the same accommodation exchange website through which I had met Mel the American.

Noel and Di were both clergy – Noel a recently retired pastor and Di a hospital chaplain – and I got a wonderful vibe from their friendly, introductory email before they stayed with me a year or so previously. Their eldest daughter Jo had done the traditional Aussie pilgrimage of leaving for the UK to work for a year or two, and was now teaching in Cambridge in the south of England. Noel and Di were going to be over for a few weeks visiting Jo and doing a grand tour of the UK, and the three of them stayed with me in Inverness for a couple of nights.

They were a pleasure to host and I got on well with them, and they insisted they returned the favour if I made it down under. They loved my mullet idea, and although they'd never heard of Mullet Creek Noel promised to look into it for me when they returned home.

I gave them the rough location. 'It looks from the map to be roughly halfway between Brisbane and Rockhampton,' I'd said, picking two of the few place names marked on the map I'd found online.

Noel looked back at me blankly. 'Simon,' he said earnestly, 'That's over a thousand miles of coastline.'

Ah, I thought. Australia was going to be a totally different kettle of fish to the Ireland trip, and indeed anything else I had experienced before. Mullets would be hard to find in such a big place, but at least I would have friends to help.

The second reason I decided Australia would be next was that, by accident, I found a second Mullet Creek there. While googling for information about Mullet Creek in Queensland (which was proving as difficult to find as a dry armpit at a ceilidh), I came across a photograph in Google Images of a cow being rescued from a stream, and the caption referred to the location as Dapto.

I googled Dapto, and found that it was a town in the Australian state of New South Wales and appeared to be a couple of hours south of Sydney. This other Mullet Creek –

from what I could make out – was literally just that, a creek, running along the edge of Dapto.

Great, I thought. Two mullets in one country – that would make the trip all the more worthwhile, significantly reducing both the miles and pounds per mullet. I looked at a map of Australia online and checked out where the two Mullet Creeks were. Mullet Creek, somewhere just north of Bundaberg on the Queensland coast; and Mullet Creek, just south of Sydney on the New South Wales coast. Sure, they were hundreds of miles apart on the east coast of Australia, but it was just a couple of inches on my computer screen. No worries, as the Aussies would say.

That, then, was the day that one of the great classic overland journeys was born – Dapto to Bundaberg.

I began saving money for the air fare, negotiated with my boss to take extra leave, and starting planning a six-week adventure in Australia for the summer of 2005.

I had a problem though. Two mullets, not very much information. One option was to just pitch up and see what I could find, but that lack of preparation had almost led to trouble in Albania, and I didn't want to run that risk on the other side of the world. Besides, I wasn't even sure I knew exactly where the northern Mullet Creek was, other than just north of Bundaberg. I needed help – local help.

Then I remembered my unimpressed browsing through the local newspaper in Ballina on my way to Belmullet, and how my trip was arguably as big a story as much of the local news it contained.

Of course, I thought to myself, the local media! A few emails to a few newspapers or radio stations, and the information would come flooding in – but did I really have enough to catch the attention of journalists? I figured I needed something more than just an idea, a mission. I needed somehow to . . . embody it. Have a point of reference.

I decided to make a website.

I'm not much of a technological guru by nature, but did know how to make a very, very basic website – just some text, the odd photo or two, and maybe if I pushed myself a coloured background, but nothing too snazzy. I bought myself a web domain name, www.simonvarwell.co.uk, and began designing my online home.

After a week or two of punching my computer screen, phoning knowledgeable friends at very antisocial hours, and some very boring, very eye-straining code-writing on my computer, I eventually had something resembling a semi-respectable presence on the internet. I didn't put up much, though – just a little introduction to me, a description and pictures of some of my past travels, plus of course all the background about the mullet mission with a big, plaintive appeal for both new mullets and information about the ones I already knew about.

From that, I had a launch pad. I started with the Queensland Mullet Creek, and tracked down the Bundaberg News-Mail, which appeared to be the local newspaper. I wrote an email to the editor, asking for help and information. I didn't explicitly ask if she would like to consider publishing an appeal or doing a story about the mission, but between the lines I certainly felt my email said 'this is quirky, give it a second look!'

Instead, I got a rather dismissive email back a couple of days later:

'As far as I am aware Mullet Creek includes a small group of houses and has a creek. It is really unimpressive as far as I know.

I can not imagine stopping there for any reason . . . (let alone travelling from anywhere else to get there)
Regards
Lucy Ardern
Editor'

Well, that wasn't much help. No gleeful pouncing on the story of the century, nor any particularly useful information or even a mere 'good luck'. The brevity of the email, however, just increased my thirst for facts, and drove me to ask around elsewhere.

I tried one step higher – the state-wide newspaper, the Brisbane Courier-Mail (incidentally, did all Australian newspapers have double-barrelled names?). I got an email back from a journalist called Rod Chester, who was more positive but ultimately less informative:

Hi Simon
i'm afraid i'm no help when it comes to info about Mullet Creek – never knew it existed until now. You might find the Bundaberg tourism folk have something to offer – http://www.bundabergregion.info/.

But let me know when you're in our area – you sound mad enough to be worth a story to me
cheers
Rod Chester
The Courier-Mail

Mad? What was mad about wanting to travel to the other side of the world to visit a location I knew nothing about, except that it was named after a bad haircut?

Honestly.

Well, at least he hadn't closed the door entirely on helping me in the future, so next I hit the Bundaberg tourist website. No mention of Mullet Creek as one of the top destinations (or for that matter on a list of really unimpressive places not worth travelling to), so I sent them an email asking for help, and got this reply:

'Good Afternoon Simon
Thank you for your enquiry
Mullet Creek is near Miriam Vale which is a small town north of Bundaberg

Please see our web site for more information
Kind Regards
Hilda Schmidt
Visitor Information Services'

See your website? Gee, thanks Hilda – that's where I got your bloody email address. But at least she'd given me something a bit more useful, and had allowed me to track Mullet Creek down more precisely on an internet map to forty kilometres northwest of Bundaberg. There were a few dots nearby including one on a railway line that appeared to run through the area. This still left me with no basic facts about the place, though – its size, its population, or the prevalence of mullet haircuts. Not even an offer of help by way of a public appeal for information.

Maybe there really was nothing there. Or maybe . . . maybe it was some fantastic, out of this world location, so wonderful that the locals wanted to keep it to themselves? Or maybe it sheltered a dark, sordid secret, and everyone including the tourist authorities and media, closed ranks and pulled over a veil of secrecy whenever an unwanted outsider threatened its privacy? I had visions of some sort of Wicker Man-style pagan community, where prying busybodies such as I would get barbecued by sinister mullet-wearing rugby players who called me 'mate' as I burned slowly to death.

Stranger things have happened, after all.

Oh alright, they probably haven't.

Although I wasn't getting anywhere with Queensland's Mullet Creek, others were, unbeknown to me at the time, making progress on my behalf. My new website had started to receive a bit of interest, particularly from among friends and acquaintances, many of whom had taken on the mantle of the mission personally.

One friend emailed to say she'd found a mullet one hundred and ninety feet below sea level in California in the USA. No, not a fish, but an island – Mullet Island, which due to rising sea levels seemed to have been depopulated. Another friend sent me a link referring to a place in Haiti called Mullet.

I was intrigued by an island that was below sea level. How would I get there? By submarine? I didn't look much more closely however, because Mullet in Haiti sounded equally interesting.

Haiti, I knew, was a former French colony in the Caribbean and so Mullet would probably be pronounced something like 'mooll-*eh*', as in femme mullée. Excellent. That sounded exotic. What wasn't exotic or even faintly appealing, though, was the fact that Haiti was in a state of virtual civil war following a military coup. There was random violence, killings and extreme political instability. The British Foreign and Commonwealth Office's travel advice for the country was as follows:

'We advise against all but essential travel to Haiti, because of the threat to personal security. There are incidences of violence and kidnappings for ransom, with kidnappings taking place mainly in Port-au-Prince.'

It was a far cry from Mullet Bay in St Martins, the other Caribbean mullet which was one of the very first I'd found. St Martins, I'd discovered, was a beautiful, prosperous island, one half owned by France and the other by the Netherlands, and it was a major tourist destination. Haiti, although being in the same rough area, could not have been any more different.

Niall wrote from South Korea, however, to tell me about a slightly more peaceful mullet he'd found: Mullet Hall Plantation, a farm in South Carolina in the USA on which slaves had been set to work. It appeared to have been in operation before slavery's abolition in the nineteenth century and from what I could make out, its past had been thoroughly researched by historians interested in that dark era.

Three new mullets and I hadn't even made it to Australia yet!

If that wasn't enough, my own research of Mullet Creeks in

Australia had led to a result that for some strange reason mentioned the Falkland Islands. Intrigued, I refined my Google search to look for a Mullet Creek in the Falkland Islands and, true enough, I'd found myself another mullet, nestled somewhere in that curious British outpost in the far South Atlantic.

North Carolina. Under water in California. Haiti. The Falkland Islands. Just as I was looking at Australia, the Americas were fighting back with four new contributions. This mission was getting bigger than I could have imagined.

EIGHT

World Mullet Tour

I liked the idea of visiting the Falkland Islands. I – like probably most British people – only knew about it because of the war in 1982 when Argentina laid claim to the 3,000 people and tens of thousands of sheep, and it took a hastily-prepared British military force to travel to the other side of the world and repel the invasion. The war was short but nasty. I knew very little else about the Falklands apart from the windswept location, sheep and soldiers. It sounded rather like Benbecula with penguins.

With just a few months before my voyage to Australia, I should have been focussed on the mullets I was heading for, but the Falkland Islands lingered in my mind. One day I was thinking about the islands, and so I tracked down the local rag, the delightfully-named Penguin News, and sent off an email. A response came back within a day.

'Dear Simon,

Mullet Creek is only a couple of miles south of Stanley so is easy to get to.

If you need further information, you could try contacting International Tours and Travel Ltd. Their email address is jf.itt@horizon.co.fk

Best wishes
Jenny Cockwell
Editor'

I loved how Jenny described herself as editor. I didn't doubt her, but given the small population of Falkland, I assumed we weren't talking about a global media empire. I imagined Jenny probably also doubled up as home affairs correspondent, graphic designer, sports reporter, stapler-in-chief, and the lady who made the tea. Editorial meetings would be wonderfully swift.

Many small island communities were like this, relying on people doubling up in different jobs. During the years I grew up in Benbecula, the local undertaker was also the coal merchant: had there been a crematorium on the island, I expect its operations would have been highly efficient.

I also loved how Jenny managed to get a sell in for a local tour company. It was probably operated by her brother. Or Jenny herself, perhaps while simultaneously running the post office, pub, airport traffic control centre, and secondary school.

She seemed amenable, so I tapped off a response, hoping to exploit her readership:

Dear Jenny
Many thanks for your mail – I do appreciate your help.If and when my Falklands leg happens, I might get back in touch with you, if it is not too cheeky of me. It might be a story for you!
Kind regards
Simon

Back came Jenny's reply, within a day:

Simon,

One extra point of interest (which may be a little too overwhelming for you!), there's a guy who lives here who has the unfortunate nickname of Mullet.

Not sure whether it's due to a hairstyle or if it's because he has the expression of a fish . . .

Jenny

I can tell you now that it was only the fact that I'd already booked my flight to Australia which prevented me changing my journey right there and then.

The boost I got from Jenny at Penguin News made me redouble my efforts on the Australian media front. I hadn't contacted the media in Dapto because I knew that Mullet Creek's location, and it didn't seem too out of the way for me to find my own way around. However, I still was keen to get more information, so tracked down the regional paper, the Illawarra Mercury (only a single-barrelled title here) and sent off an email:

Warm greetings from the Highlands of Scotland.

I am going to be in Wollongong this July with the purpose of visiting Mullet Creek. This is part of my ongoing mission to visit all the places in the world that have the word 'mullet' in their name. There are eleven that I know of, and there are two that I will be 'bagging' in Australia this summer. I wonder if this is an anecdote worthy of your publication.

But more than that, I'd be grateful to know of any information about Mullet Creek — it's been very hard to find out much about it other than its location and the fact that the emergency services were once photographed pulling a cow out of it. If any of your readers live near its banks or know anything of its history, or perhaps the origins of its name, or indeed if there is a prevalence of mullet haircuts there, I would be grateful to hear from them. You can discover more about my mission at www.simonvarwell.co.uk.
With thanks and best wishes
Simon

I'm not sure what I got right with that email, but I got a lovely response from a journalist called David Braithwaite the next morning at work:

G'day Simon,

I've been handed the prize assignment (I'm not taking the mickey –
my other story today is about rail patronage) of replying to your
e-mail. We're very (probably unreasonably) interested in promoting
your mullet-centred quest, and would like to line up an interview at
your convenience. Our resident world time experts have calculated
you're about nine hours behind over/up there, so maybe we could
give you a bell first thing in the morning Aussie time, which would
be about midnight for you? If that proves too disruptive to your
healthy Highlands sleep patterns, we can always do an e-mail
interview. We'd also like a pic of yourself to go with the story – I'm
assuming you're simply paying homage to mullets and don't actually
have one, so maybe near a recently visited mullet-related sign?
Anyway, looking forward to hearing from you.

Yours in dubious hairdo's,
Dave.

p.s A colleague who's done a Scottish tour of duty and checked out
your website said to ask you how the Ross County football side's
doing?

Brilliant. Dave was enthusiastic, funny, understood the dubious nature of the mullet, was keen to do a plug, and he even
knew about the mighty Ross County. Plus, he started his email
'G'day'. Nice and authentic. Excited, I instantly sent off a
reply:

Good morning Dave

(and I assume it will be morning there too by the time you read this,
unless you are working late – in which case, my sympathies)

Thanks for your mail and your interest. Yes, just to confirm, I do not
have a mullet. I am not sure if homage is the right word – more a

grudging respect. Although above all, I think the adventure is borne out of boredom more than anything else.

Timing of an interview – we are on British Summer Time right now (not that you'd tell from the weather), which is one hour ahead of GMT. Between 9 and 5 (roughly) I can be found at work, on +44 1463 ******, but no guarantee that I will able to talk freely or phone you back or anything.

My suggestion therefore is that you either phone me at 8am our time tomorrow (which should just about be 5pm on Thursday for you?) or even better, any time around midnight or 1am tonight (your early Thursday morning), because I really don't function well before lunchtime! My number is +44 1463 ******. Look forward to speaking to you later.

As for pictures, I'll see what I can email you after work this evening when I get home.

With best wishes, and enjoy the rail story!

Simon

PS Ross County are doing what they do best – mediocrity that steers a neat course between noteworthy and disappointing. They are towards the top of the first division but are unlikely to be good enough for promotion to the premier league for at least a couple of years. They have the unique distinction in British football of having achieved an attendance (6,000) higher than the population of their home town (Dingwall: pop 5,000), which occurred when they drew Rangers at home in the cup a few years ago. There's something for your next dinner party!

Late that night, early the next morning for him, Dave phoned me and interviewed me about the mission and my appeal for information. That Saturday, the article was published.

Then over the weekend, the emails started coming in . . .

Hello Simon, read the attached story about your proposed adventure researching all things Mullet. What a fantastic idea, sure beats lazing around the pool at some 5 star resort getting bored.

Anyway I have a business which adjoins Mullet creek at Dapto NSW Australia, not nearly as majestic as that stretch shown in the paper, we are a little upstream and unfortunately have a few weeds and bloody noxious willow trees (are they English? perhaps you could take them back with you).

You would be very welcome to visit us at the Mountain Range Nursery www.mountainrange.com.au and we could probably find a bed (caravan) for you for a couple of days if required.

Dapto is a suburb of Wollongong but I guess you have done your research and know all that.

cheers
Lance Carr

I liked Lance instantly, despite holding a Scotsman responsible for English trees – not only for his kind offer of a bed, but for his appreciation of my mission. He saw it not as the whacky result of a bored guy with too much time and imagination (though he'd not have been far wrong if he'd said so) but as way of having a holiday with a difference. He was right: I'm sure I'd have got bored of a 5 star hotel within a day or two, and a conventional holiday would never take me to unusual places like Dapto, Belmullet or Mullet in Albania. I opened Lance's attachment, which was a copy of the newspaper article he'd kindly taken the time to scan for me. I got a buzz as I read the headline:

'World Mullet Tour: Next Stop Illawarra'

Above the headline was a photo of me and a photo of a roadsign bearing those magical words: Mullet Creek. At last. Visible proof it was really there. I knew from that moment I wouldn't really feel like I'd arrived until I'd photographed that roadsign myself.

I skim-read the article, a grin creeping across my face as I went:

By DAVID BRAITHWAITE

The pioneers who founded Mullet Creek near Dapto could never have imagined it would one day share its name with an infamous hairstyle. But this cruel twist of fate will next month be highlighted by a Scotsman on a quest to visit every place on the planet with 'mullet' in its name. Inspired by travels through one of the hairstyle's last natural habitats, Eastern Europe, Simon Varwell, 26, is taking his mullet-mania to the world.

The globetrotting mullet fan will visit Lake Illawarra's Mullet Creek early next month, before a trip to its Queensland namesake, near Bundaberg. Mr Varwell blamed a dull afternoon, internet and 'silliness' for his expedition, which has so far taken him to the village of Belmullet in Ireland.

'I was surfing the net at work one day, found five places around the world with mullet in their name and it's all gone silly from there,' he said. 'I know of about 12 mullet places now – I'm not sure what I'll find when I reach them, but as long as I get a photo with the signs I'll be happy.'

Mr Varwell said the mullet, popularised in the West by 1980s icons such as David Hasselhoff and John Stamos, still thrives in former Soviet states. He said the style has evolved beyond a short top and long, flowing back into new versions such as the balding 'skullet' and woman's 'femmullet'. Varwell, who sports a sensible short back and sides, claims the mullet's ultimate expression comes from the land hair fashion forgot: Albania.

'I did my post-uni travels with a friend called Niall in 2001, where we basically went overland from Frankfurt to Cairo,' Varwell said. 'Niall's always been a bit of a mullet-spotter and he started a mullet-league table by recording sightings and giving them a rating out of 100. 'I kind of got swept up by it all and got hooked – places like Prague were good, but the best was a Northern Albanian town called Shkodra. 'It was fantastic for mullets, we saw really long rat-tails and very fluffy perms, but the best was a dwarf femmullet – a very short lady with a mullet.'

Anyone able to help Mr Varwell with information about Mullet Creek can contact him at mail@simonvarwell.co.uk.

Magnificent. Okay, he'd spelt femme mullée wrong, and I'd said 'basically' and 'kind of' too much, but it was a brilliant article nonetheless – quirky, eye-catching, to the point, and emphasising my request for help. By publishing my email address, though, he'd not just caused Lance to drop a line with his kind offer of accommodation. Other correspondents from the Dapto area got in touch too . . .

hey my name is shona, i live in dapto which is near mullet creek in the illawarra, new south wales australia. be warned not to go swimming in the creek as the farmers tend to dispose of their animal carcuses in their, it is very dirty, n also people like to have sex on the banks. when do usuppose u will be there? ok see yah

– – – –

Hello my name is Tarra. I found A place that contains the word mullet. It is called mullet creek. It is in Dapto NSW Australia. But the water is gross. Why do you have a fascination with the word mullet?
G2G
Tarra

Clearly punctuation left something to be desired among some of Dapto's citizens. As did basic logic, as Tarra proved by emailing me to tell me about the existence of a mullet I had emailed the local newspaper about, her perusal of which being her very reason for emailing me.

There was more, too . . . it seemed that Dapto had already achieved some degree of fame:

Besides Mullet Creek near Dapto, perhaps someone might shout you a viewing of the film Mullet, which was filmed in the Illawarra. The props have been taken away, including the mocked up toilet at the end of the verandah of the house which was used in the film. During the filming one elderly lady visitor mistook the toilet mockup for the real thing and emerged somewhat ruffled after the producer had hammered on the door shouting 'Don't flush!'

P Ferguson

– – – –

hey,i jsut read an insane story about you and ur mullet quest in the illawarra mercury (wollongong australia), just wanna let u know that thats heaps kool!! and while ur here in the gong make sure u check out 'mullet' – the movie which was shot in town bout 5 years ago . . . im in it as an extra in afooty game . . . . cheers
-matt

A film called Mullet! Filmed near Mullet Creek! I made a mental note to hunt the film down when I got to Australia.

Then I received a delightful email from a man called David . . .

I read about your interest in things Mullet and your planned visit to Mullet Creek at Dapto just south of Wollongong, New South Wales, Australia. I live in Kiama which is about 40 kms south of Wollongong and about 30 kms south of Mullet Creek.

I think our Mullet Creek would have been named after the Mullet fish which would live there. Creek is the term that Australians use for any waterway which is not a river as stream, brook etc are not really used here.

I thought of something which may interest you – a post card of Mullet Creek Dapto. Mullet Creek is very ordinary looking, as you will see (or have seen) and not a place for tourists or postcards today. It so happens I collect old postcards and almost 100 years ago a postcard of Mullet Creek was produced. If you would like an original post card I can post you one as I have a spare one.

A one hundred year old Mullet Creek postcard! Good grief! Now that was something I never thought I would possess. But David went on: he'd heard of the film too:

There was a film called 'Mullet' produced in this district about 5 years ago. I have also attached 2 scans from my DVD copy of that film. The film was made mainly in Kiama but some filmed at Wollongong. I don't think any was filmed at Mullet Creek. The film is about a young fellow whose nick name is Mullet and who returns to his home town after a few years away but he finds it hard to get along with his family & old friends. He also catches Mullet fish in a creek but it is a fish that no one wants and is difficult or impossible to sell. He has long hair – see the picture but I am not exactly sure if it fits the definition of a Mullet haircut. (I thought a pony tail may be necessary). This film is probably still obtainable on DVD. I could inquire if it interests you.
David

I loved how David had gone to all the effort of scanning in copies of the DVD cover and giving me a plot synopsis. It almost removed the need for me to watch the film myself.

A wonderfully random, and above all incredibly informative, set of emails had come out of Dave's excellent article. The power of the media, eh? I was so glad I had approached the Mercury. I replied to all the mails I got with polite thanks, taking Lance up on his kind offer of accommodation, and David up on the postcard.

I also knocked off a quick email to Dave at the Mercury to thank him for his help and tell him about the response the article had generated, and also update him on my travel plans as he was keen to do a follow-up article once I reached Dapto.

However, quite possibly the most incredible email I got on the back of the article appeared in my inbox. It didn't really tell me anything I didn't already know, but was still utterly, bizarrely, compelling:

Hi Simon

We read in our local paper you were coming to Mullet Creek in Dapto on your mullet quest. Paul has a much loved mullet that he's had since the early 80s. (Much to the kids disgust.) They have brought him the Mullet album and give me hell about his 80s fashion constantly. We would like to know when you will be visiting Mullet Creek so we can help a fellow appreciator of the stylish Mullet in your quest.

All kidding aside, Paul would love a photo with you to tease the kids.

Please email us if we can help you with any local history of Mullet Creek, Paul has lived here all his life.

Tanya and Paul

Did I want to meet a man with a mullet? At Mullet Creek?
It sounded too hideous to resist.

My trip to Australia was going to run from the last few days in
June until early August. Just over five weeks, all of which
would be spent, thankfully, in Australia's winter, when temperatures would plunge perilously down towards such freezing
temperatures as twenty degrees Celsius.

The provisional plan was to fly into Sydney and spend a few
days there on either side of a two-day trip to Dapto. Then I
would work my way up the coast towards Brisbane, head
further north to Mullet Creek by Bundaberg, then return to
Brisbane to fly home.

Following the media work, my attention turned to arranging
accommodation. Towards the end of my trip I would be
staying with Noel and Di in Brisbane, and as I worked my
way north from Sydney I would just grab whatever hostels I
could find.

Starting out with a few days in Sydney, however, led me to
see what the accommodation exchange website had to offer.
After all, I'd hosted numerous times in Inverness and figured it
might be nice to see how the network felt from the other side of
the bargain.

So I scribbled off an email and sent it to as many of the
hundreds of Sydney-registered members as I felt I could get away
with. It was a tough job – I had to be concise, make myself sound
interesting and friendly, and convince complete strangers to open
their homes to me. I realised now how hard it must have been for
other users to have contacted me. In the end, I found some words
that I felt projected a clean, decent image, while at the same time
catching readers' eyes with the details of the mission:

Hello!

My name is Simon, I am 26, and come from Inverness, in the
Highlands of Scotland. I write this with some trepidation. Although I

have hosted many times, this is the first time I have attempted to use the site to seek accommodation elsewhere!

I am flying into Sydney on the 29th of June, and would hope to spend three or four days exploring your fine city, before heading onwards to Mullet Creek, Wollongong. My visit to Australia is a five-week tour, a major part of my ongoing mission to visit all the places in the world that have the word 'mullet' in their name (two of which are in Australia).

I am fairly relaxed and easy-going, and am a non-smoker. I am single, Christian and have (I think) a good sense of humour. I am a keen pubber but can last surprisingly long without a pint. I work for a federal university in Inverness, a job which takes me all over the Highlands of Scotland and beyond. You can find out more about me at my website – www.simonvarwell.co.uk.

Through the site I have really enjoyed meeting people from other parts of the world, especially Australians who seem to be more proud of their country than any other nationality I have come across! I am a keen reader, walker and traveller, having done much of Europe. This will be my first trip down under.

With thanks and very best wishes
Simon

And I waited. But just like the Mercury article, I didn't need to wait too long for the responses to start coming in.

Gday Simon,

Would have loved to help but unfortunately I am not home in Oz at the moment. Currently backpacking Europe and then Canada. Off to Canada for a year to go do Whistler :)

Sinista Vila

I had no idea what 'doing Whistler' involved (it sounded rather kinky, to be honest), or whether Sinista Vila was a real name –

but never mind, a cheery response. And others came in quickly too:

Hey Simon, how are you?Thanks for the e-mail and it's good that you're coming over to Australia. Sydney is a good place to start and Wollongong is a nice town to visit.Unfortunately I'm going travelling myself this summer. I will go home to Indonesia in June and then I'm off to the UK for 2 years working holiday, so I won't be in Sydney when you get here.
Yohannes

— — — —

Hi Simon
Unfortunately I'll be flying out to the Uk from the 14th of June for a few months so I can't host this time but if you have any questions about sydney I'll try and help you out.
Cheers Andy

— — — —

Hi Simon,

Your quest to visit places that have the word 'mullet' in them is one I can only wholeheartedly admire. You should be aware that two places in Sydney have their own special mullet: the suburbs of Newtown and Paddington, from where the unimaginatively named 'Newtown mullet' and 'Paddington mullet' spring from. But I digress.

I would have loved to host you but alas, I am currently overseas myself and thus cannot. I hope you find somewhere to stay in Sydney, and meet many Australians who are *not* proud of their country, as there's not a lot to be proud of at the moment!

Cheers,
Gigi Adair

Gigi Adair? Did Australia specialise in exotic names, or something?

hi simon.
i'll actually be in edinburgh for a family wedding! not quite as far
north as inverness but getting there.not sure if you know named
jamie barker? inverness lad, now living in sydney. might be
worth dropping him a line if you do.sorry i can't help out on this
occasion.

david.

Yes David, we all know each other in Inverness and are all, in
fact, related. Hang on and I'll just nip into the next room to
pass on your regards to his family.

gday simon,

great intro letter . . . and unfortunately i won't be able to host you
because i am heading off to brazil.

such a shame cos i think your mission to visit places called mullet it
tops! i had a mullet myself once . . . a hair modelling disaster, i said
do anything except a mullet, and they did an assymetrical mullet.
nice one.

i have hosted more than i'v been hosted, but it's an awesome
experience, and i'd rather take in people who have hosted before
than those that haven't, you'll have no lack of offers i'm sure.

cheers and have an awesome time!

/Geri

– – – –

so sorry mate but im actually in alaska at the moment and wont be home till christmas. but have an awesome time!!!

simone

— — — —

Simon,

Unfortunately, I will be in the UK myself when you are here. Enjoy your stay down under.

Lainie

— — — —

Hi Simon,

Very sorry we can't host you at the time you'll be in Sydney (we are in India). I'm sure we would have liked to meet someone who is chasing places named 'mullet'???? Can go mullet fishing in our neighbourhood – they're quite delicious . . .

Dave & Dee

— — — —

HI SIMON . JUST A REALLY QUICK HELLO , AND TO LET YOU KNOW THAT IAM IN THE USA AT THE MOMENT , AND WILL NOT BE HOME TILL DEC 2005, SO IAM SORRY , MAY BE NEXT YEAR IF YOU ARE AROUND , BYE FOR NOW DES

. . . I'm sure you get the point: overeager, overfriendly, and overseas. I should have guessed that would be the case, Australia being a nation of such insatiable travellers. In fact, given the numbers of Australians pulling pints throughout the

UK, and the legions that I'd met travelling in Eastern Europe, I couldn't help thinking that Australia really ought to just shut up shop and leave a big sign at the major entry points saying 'Out for a while; back in a few years.'

Thankfully though, there was a lovely collection of responses from folk who hadn't left the country and who were happy to either put me up or meet up for a pint. The first positive respondents were a New Zealand couple called Tara and Pete, who agreed to host me for a couple of days when I arrived. There was a lady called Christine, originally from Newcastle in England, who said she'd take me in; and an easygoing guy called Benj asked me to help him housesit for some friends who were on holiday. Then a handful of other responses from lots of other really nice sounding people made for a nice warm pre-welcome to Australia.

I ended up exchanging quite a few emails with them all in the days leading up to my departure, and I mentioned to Christine how sociable and friendly everyone had been. She replied suggesting that I organise a night out for all the Sydney folk I was in touch with.

A Scotsman? A night out? I could do that!

I was all set to go. I'd located the two mullets, whipped up interest in Dapto, and awoken a band of lovely people in Sydney to kick off my trip.

Australia awaited: at least one journalist, a farmer with a caravan, information from a vintage postcard collector and other randoms, several friendly people to stay with, and around 1,000 miles of road to cover.

Oh yes, and a bloke with a mullet whose wife wanted a photo of me with him.

It was bound to be an adventure . . .

NINE

Sidneysiders

Australia clearly knew there was a Scotsman coming to visit, as it was raining when I arrived. It was early on a Friday morning in late June, the middle of Sydney's pathetic attempt at a winter. It was only half past six in the morning, so that gave me a welcome chance to freshen up.

Never having travelled such a long distance before, I'd probably made the worst possible preparation for a long-haul flight. The day before I left the UK, I had flown down to London and stayed with friends for the night. The next day, I wandered around town doing some last minute shopping and catching a quiet pint in the mid-afternoon with my friends. It was a roasting hot summer's day and, by the time I had survived a day of Oxford Street and the stuffy Underground trip to Heathrow airport, I was drenched in sweat. Moreover, I'd stupidly dressed in jeans and trainers, which I could feel were beginning to cling to me and exude distinct aromas all of their own.

Then we were delayed in departing London, so when we arrived in Singapore after a relatively uneventful flight, my intended two hour stopover became a thirty second sprint across the humid terminal to the departure lounge for Sydney. When I flopped down in my seat in the cramped economy class, I apologised instantly to the amiable Taiwanese gentleman next to me. He was very sympathetic to my heat intolerance – he'd never been to Scotland, but most of what he'd heard involved very cold weather.

After arriving at Sydney and making good use of the showers at the airport, I felt much better. Though till a bit groggy after two sleepless flights, I was changed, cleaned, and ready to explore the southern hemisphere.

I headed to the airport's railway station, and invested in a seven day pass for the suburban rail network, figuring that it would take me that time to explore Sydney and meet all the people I'd connected with from the accommodation exchange website.

First of those was Tara, my host for the next couple of nights, who had instructed me to meet her at her office – a legal practice in the centre of Sydney – where I would be able to dump my bags for the day. Tara was bright, cheerful, breezy and very chatty. She also had a pronounced New Zealand accent, still strong despite eighteen years in Sydney.

I usually have a good ear for accents, and am proud of the fact that I can distinguish an Australian from a New Zealander, thanks to advice from a New Zealander I'd met in Istanbul. He explained that, as with many accents, there was a key phrase that helped make distinctions, in this case 'twenty-six fish and chips' – the Australians pronounce the vowels clearly and roundly, while their neighbours across the sea would say 'twunny-sux fush and chups', dragging the vowels along the ground behind them.

In the same way, I discovered some months later, 'out and about in a boat' can separate Canadians from Americans: Americans generally have an unremarkable pronunciation to the British ear, while their cousins to the north render it 'ewt and abewt in a boot'.

Meanwhile, you've maybe not heard the story of the man from the island of North Uist who travelled through Benbecula to visit South Uist, where you can often hear distinct pronunciations of the 'th' sound.

Upon arrival in South Uist, the visitor got stuck in a peat bog.

'I'm sinking, I'm sinking!' he cried out to a passing local.

'Well, that's great,' came the relaxed reply. 'Now tell me what you're sinking about.'

'Yis, I've nivver minudged to shake ut off', Tara replied, while drawing me a map of the immediate area. I was grateful for her help, as I have an atrocious sense of direction. However, I was to find over my time in Sydney that it was an easy city to negotiate, and the rail network would prove to be excellent – reliable, good value, and regular, all novelties for a Scottish traveller.

Armed with Tara's map and my Lonely Planet guide, I headed off to explore Sydney for the day.

The excitement of a new country and new city meant I kept relatively bright and awake throughout the day despite the lack of sleep. I was also refreshed by the light, warm rain – which most Sydneysiders (as I was led to believe was the collective noun) seemed to have responded to with thick winter coats and umbrellas as big as parachutes that I swear were brought out with the sole intention of trying to poke out my eyes. I, on the other hand, was dressed in sturdy sandals, light cotton trousers and a short-sleeved shirt, and was positively basking in the fresh, cool air.

I started my exploration just a couple of blocks from Tara's office, at Circular Quay. This was the picture postcard centre of Sydney which boasted the Opera House, the harbour bridge, and a bustling pier where you could get ferries to other parts of the city and which was littered with buskers and colourful street performers. It was enclosed by the central business district, the Botanic Gardens, and The Rocks, the 'historic' old part of Sydney.

The Rocks was very pretty, with boutiques, bars, and tourist shops serving as evidence that this was a beautifully regenerated area and an artsy and bohemian centre of nightlife and culture. However, a small museum just up the hill, dating from the 1860s, boasted that it was one of Sydney's oldest buildings. I allowed myself a smug, European, laugh – I'd grown up in a house only just younger than that.

Moreover, I thought to myself as I stood on the hill and looked over the bustling quay, the Opera House seemed a peculiarly bland building. Far from being an icon of modern architecture that it was feted as, I couldn't help noticing its . . . well, ugliness. It made Inverness's Eden Court Theatre look beautiful, which really is saying something. As for the harbour bridge, it was not that imposing, and reminded me of a similar one in Newcastle.

I'd barely arrived in Australia, and was already falling into a trap I normally manage to avoid. I have learned over the years never to travel with high expectations or demands, and try to simply enjoy whatever is thrown at me. When Niall and I completed our epic journey in 2001, we went to visit the pyramids of Giza, one of the seven ancient wonders of the world and probably the most iconic images of Egypt, if not the whole of Africa.

They were deeply, deeply disappointing.

I'd expected long treks through deserts and sandstorms to tall, imposing, mysterious buildings that emitted a low-frequency 'ommmmm' if you listened closely. I'd wanted to enter the pyramids and navigate dark labyrinths in which our flame torches would mysteriously blow out, hieroglyph-covered walls would move upon the lightest touch to reveal secret chambers, and where we would walk down eerie, cobwebbed corridors only for the members of our party bringing up the rear to inexplicably vanish; before we fought our way through armies of flesh-eating beetles to reach vast caverns filled with coins, jewellery and mummified remains of Pharaohs.

Sure, none of that was promised in the guidebook, but it still disappointed me that the reality was completely different: much smaller pyramids than I'd expected, and interiors consisting of short, straight passageways at the end of which stood a tour guide with outstretched hands in anticipation of a generous tip.

Having travelled for four months towards a single destination, though, you sometimes can't help building up hopes; and this is why I'd come to Sydney harbouring barely any, other than an expectation that I'd have a pretty good time. With few expectations, I reasoned, I would never be disappointed.

I figured, therefore, that my uncharacteristic cynicism after just a few hours of Sydney was just due to being a bit weary from the flight, and told myself to cheer up.

I took an amble across the quayside. Under the shadow of gleaming, modern tower blocks, I walked through bustling crowds of commuters and tourists, past rows of ferries docked to load and unload cargoes of crowds.

The centre of Sydney sat as if in the palm of a hand with many outstretched fingers, which were mostly lush, tree-lined and home to the better off. With such a circuituitous coastline, ferry trips were a more direct route into the heart of the city than going overland.

By the row of ferries, I was distracted by the catchy beat of a street musician. An Aboriginal guy in traditional costume was squatted on the ground, playing a didgeridoo to an electronic dance beat emanating from a stereo. A small crowd was forming, and a few people were nodding their heads appreciatively in time to the music.

It was a great sound. The continuous drone of the didgeridoo perfectly suited the soft, regular rhythm of the backing track, creating a compelling blend of old and new music. Quite a few traditional musicians in Scotland had achieved much the same with bagpipes, creating popular fusions of Celtic and modern electronic sounds.

The guy with the didgeridoo paused between songs to plug his CDs, and while I was tempted buy one I resisted, figuring I'd probably think less of the sound once I was back home and listening to the music in my flat rather than here with the backdrop of Sydney's most famous architectural icons.

After listening a few more minutes I went to grab something to eat from a street vendor and headed into the Circular Quay railway station. I hopped on a train and decided to see where I ended up.

On impulse – such is the freedom of travel passes – I got off at a stop called Town Hall, largely because I had a good idea what there might be outside the station. True enough, this part of Sydney was indeed home to the very grand and imposing town hall.

Given the name of the underground stop, I joked to myself that it was probably as good a place as any to build it (bringing to mind the probably apocryphal story of the American tourist visiting Edinburgh who noted how helpful it was that they'd built the castle so close to the railway station).

Next to the town hall was the magnificent St Andrew's Cathedral. I've always been a sucker for glorious ecclesiastical architecture. Not necessarily due to cathedrals being outstanding places of worship – usually such churches have viciously uncomfortable pews, and services led by people who look like they were present at the laying of the foundation stone and have delivered the same sermon every week since then. Rather, I'm impressed by the grandeur, civic aspiration and sheer photographability of such places.

One of my favourites is the Cathedral of St Machar in the heart of Aberdeen's medieval old town. In 1495 its bishop had founded the University of Aberdeen, and the roof of the cathedral's interior is dotted with shields and crests from all across Europe – over five hundred years ago, the north of Scotland was a well-connected place. Though anyone driving along today's A96 or A9 would tell you things have notably declined in the last few centuries.

Another lovely cathedral is St Magnus' in Kirkwall, Orkney. Just off the northern mainland of Scotland, Orkney is an island group that was, like Shetland, its neighbour to the north, originally owned by Norway. Kirkwall was the capital of a major earldom, and the beautiful red stone cathedral was one of the main symbols of the town's importance. Inside, there is a compelling sense of peace and history, and names from the Viking Sagas can be found on inscriptions and windows alongside those of Orkney's more recent luminaries including a surprising wealth of famous authors.

What I really found interesting about St Andrew's as I toured its bright, cool interior – and other large, stone churches I would go on to see in Australia – was that they were all in such outstandingly good nick. Only having had a century or so of wear and tear, the exteriors were still sound, and the angles of the masonry still bold and sharp, the general appearance being one of newness. An Australian I mentioned this to later in my trip contrasted my observation with the fascination his fellow countrymen had in British cathedrals being so old, clapped out and rustic. Beauty or fascination, then, only really depended on your personal perspective.

Across the road from the town hall and the cathedral was the gorgeous Victoria Building. This was a striking, ornate shopping arcade, with numerous levels, and a quaint interior that spoke of Victorian-era grandeur mixed with an olde-worlde intimacy. Rather than the watchmakers, tea shops and craft shops my experience of Inverness's lovely Victorian Market led me to expect, Sydney's Victoria Building bustled with trendy clothes shops, delicatessens and pharmacies: lively and modern but without losing any of the ostentation.

Outside on a plinth stood an austere statue of Queen Victoria herself. According to the plaque written on it:

> *At the request of the City of Sydney, this statue of Queen Victoria was presented by the government and people of Ireland in a spirit of goodwill and friendship.*
>
> *Until 1947 it stood in front of Leinster House, Dublin, the seat of the Irish Parliament.*

This I found bizarre, and of dubious accuracy – perhaps two of the most republican parts of the former British Empire in-volved in the exchange of a monarchical statue. I imagined what the discussions preceding the handover might have been like.

'Ah now, don't ye jist tink dat it's your torn to take the old woman?'

'Streuth mate, what do we want with a haggard old Sheila like this?'

'Ah to be sure, jist hang on to her for a few years, den pass her on to someone else in the empoire . . . the Jamaicans moight take her efter yous.'

After some more exploring of the city, I made it back to Tara's office at the end of the working day, just about ready to drop. I'd been on my feet most of the day, and after a long flight I was exhausted. Tara and I caught the train back to her part of the city, a suburb west of the city centre called Panania. Despite my fighting off sleep, we talked loads on the train about travel, our experiences of hosting people through the website, and of course mullets.

Tara's family was originally from the Cook Islands, and Pete, her partner, was half-Maori. They had lived happily in Sydney since moving from New Zealand. I met Pete – and, briefly, the two dogs and three cats – when we got to their house. By now I was struggling to keep on my feet and wasn't taking in too much of my surroundings, and so Tara showed me to the guest room, where I collapsed on my bed, fell asleep, and slept deeply until 7am.

Apart, that is, from a brief moment at two o'clock in the morning, when I woke up desperate for the toilet. I edged open my bedroom door in the darkness to be greeted by the low barks of one of the dogs – I supposed I'd not spent sufficient time with them to be judged a 'friend' yet and so trying to calm the agitated one down with pats and reassuring words didn't work. I just gave up, went to the bathroom, had a pee, and came back to my room. The dog barked again, this time loudly, then the other one appeared in the dark hallway and joined in.

'Wheesht!' I hissed, to no avail. Then another dog's bark could be heard outside – the neighbours'. Within minutes, there was a cacophony of dog barking across the district, and while I'd managed to calm down my two canine hosts, it seemed the rest of Panania was going to have a sleepless night. I was amazed not to have woken Pete and Tara. I crawled back to bed, just as householders throughout the area were probably getting up, bleary-eyed, to see who was trying to break in, and fell asleep again straight away.

After sleeping over twelve hours – even with the 2am distraction – I woke up feeling nothing short of fantastic. It was a bright sunny day, I'd completely slept off the jet-lag, and over breakfast I made proper friends with the dogs and cats.

I had the house to myself, my hosts having left at the crack of dawn, Pete to his work as an electrician and Tara back to the legal practice where she worked. I was in fact to report back to Tara's office again that evening – it was the last day for a guy at her work, and Tara invited me to join in his leaving drinks.

After eating, showering and getting dressed, I went for a little explore round Panania. Seeing the area in the daylight for the first time, I found myself pretty much walking on to a scene from Aussie soap *Neighbours* – wide streets, large bungalows, 'utes' in the driveway, and cheerful-looking middle-aged people taking dogs for walks around the block. It was all reassuring and comfortable in its familiarity in one sense, but the sharp contours of the palm trees and the harsh shrieks of the unfamiliar birds contrasted with the lumbering oaks and twittering birdsong you would find in British suburbia.

The commercial centre of Panania was not much more than a hotel/bar, railway station and a couple of streets of shops, but it was pleasant enough. The shops included a post office, a couple of grocers, a pharmacy, an off-licence (though they gave them the very Australian name 'bottlos'), and a bank. The streets were quiet, with just a few people going backwards and forwards, and the sun was shining.

I was in Australia. The city was drying off after the rain, and I was going to enjoy myself.

After spending the day exploring the centre of Sydney again, I headed back to Tara's office. Out on an impressive roof balcony, eight floors up in the heart of the central business district, a party was in swing for Tara's departing colleague. It was a typical 'works do' – people milling around in groups, drinking beer, with some folk still in their suits and one or two older people wearing Hawaiian shirts as if it was the most rebellious thing they'd done for years.

Tara introduced me to a few of her colleagues, including Vaughn, a young guy who was the focus of the party – he was soon to be leaving for London, following that well-trodden migratory path for young Australians. I gave him a few wise pointers, including telling him to move north out of London as fast as he could, and wished him well. After a couple of beers, Tara led me away to another bar nearby, where we were going to meet her good friend Nat.

'So, mullets', declared Nat, as he slammed two schooners of Toohey's New down on to the table. 'This is about class, isn't it?' I took a generous slurp of my beer and relaxed in my chair. I wasn't put out by his question – Tara had warned me of his direct manner. Half New Zealander and half Fijian, Nat was shaven-headed and built like a rugby player, but gentle and amiable. He'd explained that he was, like me, a graduate of political science and international relations, so just had an inquisitive, analytical mind.

'What makes you say that?' I asked.

'You're just taking the puss out of the working cless,' he went on, his accent containing noticeably Kiwi vowels, 'because of white trailer trash. Think about it – mullets are most famous on the rednecks you get in poor rural areas of the USA and Australia.'

'Sure,' I replied, 'but that's not the reason I'm doing it. It's just a fascination with a bizarre haircut. It's got nothing to do with class. All sorts of classes sport them.'

'What does your father do?'

'He's a minister.'

'Of religion?'

'Yep.'

'That's very muddle cless, admit it.'

Nat took a drink of his beer, point made, with just the barest of smiles on his face. The three of us sipped our drinks and talked some more, including about a forthcoming holiday to Europe Nat planned. Tara, an enthusiastic hoster through the accommodation website, usually introduced any guests she had through the site to Nat, just as an extra local for folk to meet. Although at this rate most visitors to Australia would have got the impression it is populated entirely with New Zealand expatriates.

Soon, though, Tara and I departed – Pete was back in Panania at the local bar, and we were to meet him there.

The rest of the night was spent in the bar of the unimaginatively-monikered Panania Hotel, which was pretty much everything you've ever imagined about an Australian pub. Barely a woman in sight, it was full of drunk men of all ages, with wall to wall slot machines, chewing gum trodden into the carpet, and a general air of raucousness.

I'll spare you the details of the rest of the night, largely because most of them escape me – except to say that I got on great with Tara and Pete, formed a formidable acquaintance with Toohey's New; and Saturday daytime was mostly spent lying on the grass in the beautiful botanic gardens opposite the Sydney Opera House, enjoying the gentle sunshine and listening to the soothing, mellow beats of Ulrich Schnauss on my iPod.

As I lay there, though, I did think over what Nat had said the previous night about my mullet quest being a class issue. Being an islander, I'd never really grown up in a shadow of class issues, and certainly hadn't equated mulletry in Britain with the working class. A lot of mullets back home were either those awful wispy trendy ones worn by people around my own age in cool urbane bars, or hippy-derived. Plus, there wasn't really a 'white trash' culture in the same way that America or Australia had.

If Scots wanted to knock the working classes, we had the Neds – shell-suited, burberry-capped and gold-chained teenagers who thought it was unquestionably fashionable to wonder around with trousers tucked into sports socks, in clothes made out of the most flammable substance known to man. And Ned hair, far from being mulleted, was usually short, spikey and if it wasn't covered by a white baseball cap then it was a walking advert for Brylcreem.

Did Nat have a point? I was a middle class kid, I suppose, and doesn't a part of human nature criticise and find fault with those we are different from?

I dismissed the thought: clearly I'd slipped right into the slow lane of holiday mode if the most interesting thing occupying my mind was the comparative attire of various Anglo-Saxon nations' working classes.

Things were about to become livelier, however, because that night was the gathering of Sydney folk from the accommodation website, which one of them, Christine, had suggested I organise before I left. There were around half a dozen new people to meet, and my holiday was about to take a whole new direction.

I arrived early at the Orient Hotel in The Rocks. There was a rugby match on, and so I squeezed through the scrum to the thankfully not so busy bar. I found a corner, hopped on a stool, propped up the wee Scottish flag I'd brought with me for identification, and ordered a schooner of Toohey's New. I was on my own – Tara and Pete had a prior commitment with friends.

When my schooner arrived I held it in my hands. It looked and felt strange. A schooner was roughly three-quarters of a pint, Australians preferring more metric servings for their alcohol, and was the sort of serving that would warrant social scorn in most British pubs. Surely, I thought, Australians must find this a point of great national shame.

The beer was nice though. It was a warm evening, and I was slowly beginning to get used to drinking lager. Normally I would drink real ales – which Scotland does so well, and which go perfectly with dark, smoky pubs on a wild winter's evening. This, however, was Australia, where even their winter was as warm as the height of summer in the Scottish Highlands, and where a day touristing or lounging around in the sun left you needing something cooler and more refreshing than a thick, heavy pint of eighty shilling.

I sat drinking my beer, aware I was the only lone person in the bar. There were crowds of young guys watching the rugby and cheering enthusiastically, plus what I guessed were a couple of work nights out. I was at a bit of a loss – normally I'd hope to bump into someone I knew, or sit sending text messages. However I was twelve thousand miles from home and was trying to restrict my phone usage for cost reasons, so resorted to literally twiddling my thumbs and people-watching.

So many of the folk I'd emailed had been very enthusiastic about coming to the gathering tonight – not least Christine, originally from Newcastle, England, who'd suggested the meet-up and who was bringing her new flatmate. Another respondent, Benj, had seemed keen enough to squeeze in a drink or two with us before going off to a speed-dating event, and a girl called Alicia had seemed a bundle of fun from her emails. But what would they look like? What would be their characteristics? How would I recognise them? I thought about the people I'd hosted through the site – by default they were global and international in their outlook, open-minded, liberal, friendly and down to earth. Trying to put all those features on to one person, like clothes on to a manikin, all I could come up with to represent all of that was a grinning UN peacekeeper sporting a gay pride badge.

Unsurprisingly, Christine and her flatmate, the first to arrive, looked nothing like that.

Christine, who had lived in Australia for about thirty years since moving from Newcastle, spoke in a strange accent, part Geordie, part Aussie, but was warm, friendly and very chatty. Her flatmate introduced herself as Elaine.

'Hi, how ye doin'?'

'Aye, nae bad,' I laughed. 'You're Scottish!'

'Aye, ah'm fae Hamilton.'

Typical, I thought, you travel twelve thousand miles and you find someone from back home. Elaine had moved just six weeks ago from her home town near Glasgow to Sydney for a new job and a new start in life. She'd randomly found a room in Christine's house, and as fellow ex-pats, they were getting on well, Elaine already having been indoctrinated into the traveller-hosting website by Christine. Soon, I would be continuing that – due to Tara and Pete having other folk booked in from Sunday, Christine had agreed just a day or so previously by email to let me crash on her study floor for a couple of days.

We found a table upstairs in the pub, a bit further away from the noise generated by the rugby, and were soon joined by the others.

Alicia was an earnest and lively young civil servant who spent a lot of her time jetting around South East Asia for work, with whom I had exchanged quite a few emails. She was good fun, bubbly, and entertaining company. Then Benj, popping in briefly en route to his singles night, appeared, looking immensely suave and dapper, full of wise cracks and engaging anecdotes. And finally Lynne and Kevin – a lovely middle-aged couple from the suburbs of Sydney who were quiet and retiring, but full of warmth and friendliness.

As we all began chatting away, I noticed how well we were all getting on – talking about our experiences of hosting and travelling, all about where everyone came from in Sydney, and conversations carried on from my emails with them, and of course on to the subject of mullets. I also realised that I was the only person who had been in touch with everyone. Here I was on the other side of the world with a bunch of lovely people from Sydney, whose only connection with each other was through a travel website (and, more precisely, mullets), and who would not have met each other were it not for me.

We got down to ordering food, and the spirit of friendliness was soon enhanced by the spirit of a few cold lagers.

I was intrigued when I went up to the bar with my fellow Scot Elaine to find one peculiarly Australian custom – queueing to be served. Now sure, Brits love their queues, deriving an entire culture (and sometimes minor warfare) from queueing etiquette and breaches thereof. We form queues for just about every public service.

Not in pubs, though. In pubs you just throng towards the bar, push in where you can, and generally try to be aware of those who were there first in case you are offered to be served before them. Sometimes it doesn't work out fairly, and often a pretty face and captivating smile helps you bump up a few places in the order. Naturally, I find it hard to keep my place.

In Australia, however, the supposed land of beer-swilling, masculine competitiveness, everyone formed a queue – a neat line perpendicular to the bar, as if we were in the post office.

Most strange. But they served beer, and that was the main thing.

The night, although great fun, was not a wild one, and Benj had left us early for his party. I'd got on well with him, and he said I could stay with him the next weekend, once I'd returned from Dapto, my first mullet mission in Australia.

Around ten we all drifted away, and I headed back with Lynne and Kevin, who were part way down the same train line as me. We had a better chat on the train, and they told me all about the travels of their four grown-up children and the waves of folk from the website that they took into their large house. They said that knowing what it was like to travel, and then through their children, learning what it was like to be a young traveller, they really enjoyed taking in people and giving some hospitality back to those from elsewhere in the world.

I arrived back in Panania to a quiet house, the dogs greeting me as an old friend. Tired after a long day's touristing, and my body clock tricked by the dark, cool evening, I went to bed and fell soundly asleep.

The next morning I woke to find that Tara and Pete were in a slightly worse state than me. Their night out with friends had been a heavy one, finishing up back in the Panania Hotel.

Over lunch in a Chinese restaurant that afternoon, Tara and Pete told me they were seriously considering emigrating to Britain. They had lived several years in Australia and, being ready for a change, decided that Britain was the place to go. I think I made a fair impact on their thinking by tempting them away from the Antipodean fly paper that is London towards the bonnier climes of Scotland. It would have similarities to New Zealand in culture and geography, I argued, plus the likes of Glasgow or Edinburgh would give the benefits of lively city life and a thriving job market with the added bonuses of lower costs of living and easier access to the countryside than London could provide.

They seemed genuinely taken by my hard sell, so I made a mental note to ask the Scottish Government for a commission when I got back home.

Soon, though, food was over, and it was time to say thank you and goodbye to Tara and Pete. My rucksack and I hopped on a train and headed across Sydney to Artarmon, where Christine and Elaine lived.

I had enjoyed taking the train in Sydney. Partly because I was a big fan of rail travel, and partly because my week's pass meant I could travel as much as I wanted – indeed, the more I did so, the more value for money I'd get out of my pass.

It was also a great way to see the city with no effort, watching the unfamiliar cityscape going past with its dramatic, modern architecture reaching for the sky and towering over

spacious apartment buildings and large, single-storey bungalows, with not an old building in sight. It was so very different
from the cities I was used to in Europe.

At one station, a young guy got on, and as he walked down
the aisle, he stopped and spoke to me.

'Are you going swimming tonight?'

That's funny, I thought, I could have sworn he . . . I pulled
out my iPod headphones and said 'sorry?'

'Are you going swimming tonight?' I screwed my face up
in disbelief and confusion. 'Am I going . . . *swimming* tonight?'

I was met by a similar look of disbelief and confusion.

'No . . . is this going to Flemmington, mate?' he repeated
slowly, as if talking to a toddler.

I went a deep shade of red. 'Er . . . oh right, sorry, I thought
. . . er . . . no idea. I'm er . . . not from here. Sorry.'

He grunted an acknowledgement, an eyebrow raised, and
sat down as far away from me as he could. To hide my
embarrassment I suddenly found the suburban rail network
map on the wall in front of me absolutely fascinating.

And as I studied it, I actually *did* find it fascinating. I further
realised what a unique place Australia was with its ancient
indigenous cultures intermingled with peoples from all over
Britain and beyond. Among the names of train stops, unfamiliar Aboriginal tongue-twisters like Woolooware, Yagoona
and Waroonga sat alongside colonial names like Campbelltown,
MacArthur and Hamilton. To see such a famous, thriving,
modern city owe such a lot to Scotland made me feel a little
tingle of pride.

The next couple of days were spent with Christine and Elaine,
in the suburb of Artarmon. To be honest, though, it was much
the same as Panania – a street or two of the usual selection
of local shops, plus endless identical residential streets of
*Neighbours*land.

One afternoon – a Sunday – they took me out for a tour of

the local area. Elaine drove in her car, while Christine gave the guided tour from the back, insisting I sit in the passenger seat to see the scenery. We headed out to the south of the city beyond the very Australian suburbs and were soon out into winding country roads with thick forest on either side. I wondered for a moment whether it was quite like Scotland, with rolling waves of hillside and trees, but then the road signs demanding we watch out for wallabies and koalas, and the afternoon's bright winter sunshine, reminded me that I was literally on the other side of the world.

We stopped in an area called Mona Vale, whose major attraction was a huge Baha'i temple. The Baha'i faith emerged in what is now Iran a couple of centuries ago, and is unusual in that it draws on messages of all the world's major religions. I'd been to a Baha'i temple before, in the Israeli city of Haifa, an ornate walled garden and spectacular white building in the midst of it all, built in layers on a huge slope running from the top of the hill overlooking Haifa, down to sea level. It was a very dramatic (and, no doubt, massively expensive) building, and this one in Mona Vale was similar, although smaller.

We looked briefly around the adjacent visitor centre, and had a nice chat with an elderly Iranian guide who gave us a cup of tea and his life story, the latter charting his departure from Iran due to persecution for his faith, and travels across various parts of Europe. He also told us a little about his beliefs before directing us to the temple.

It was a very serene place, but its airiness and brightness made it came over to me as rather hollow and characterless. I was also intrigued to see a small bookshelf containing the Torah, the Koran and the Bible. Nothing like a bit of pic n mix to enhance your religion, I suppose.

I was surprised to learn from the Iranian gentleman that there are only seven major Baha'i temples in the world. I mentioned that I'd been to the one in Haifa.

'Well there you go,' said Elaine as we walked back to the car. 'Something to do once you're done with mullets – visit all the Baha'i temples.' Smiling at the cheeky glint in her eye, I said I'd file that idea somewhere at the back of my mind.

Our next stop was a lovely stretch of forested coastline, from which we could see across the bay to the peninsula where they filmed the other famous Aussie soap, *Home and Away*. It was a luscious-looking place, with long beaches and large houses. Apparently the property prices had gone right up when fame arrived, and it was now the preserve of the very rich.

My couple of days with Christine and Elaine were very enjoyable. It was a chance to explore more of Sydney during the day, and relax and unwind over good food, chat and a beer or two in the evenings with my hosts. I read books in peaceful parks, followed my nose on the railway network, and came to really like Sydney.

One of my expeditions was a ferry trip to Watonga, one of the numerous peninsulas on the edge of the city, which was home to Sydney zoo.

Now I'm not a huge one for zoos. I don't have any major ethical objections to them, but it's just that once you've seen one giraffe (thanks to the Blair Drummond Safari Park in Perthshire) you've seen them all. However, it was in a lovely setting, a lush green finger of land that contained not only the zoo but also leafy residential areas, a lovely coastal nature trail, and grand views back to the centre of Sydney. I followed the trail round the edge of the peninsula, taking in the different plants and animals that Australia boasted, and then when I got to the end on the other side of the peninsula I decided to cut across rather than turn back, meaning (this being me) I got spectacularly lost, and ended up wasting a couple of hours and seeing more bland suburbia and less unspoilt nature than I had intended.

Soon, though, my time in Sydney came to an end. I'd spent the best part of a week there, coming to know and like its culture, its people, its beer, and of course its rail network. The best thing was there was a bit more to come – Benj had invited me to stay later on in the week.

However, my trip was not just about doing the tourist thing in Sydney. It was about so much more than that, and after my acclimatisation to life down under it was time to get down to business. Time to head south along the coast, to Dapto.

To Mullet Creek. My first Australian 'mullet'.

TEN

Up the Creek Without a Mullet

Often the differences between two cultures aren't in the language, accent, history or music, but in the most sublime and mundane of things. For Australia and the UK, one of the big ones I noticed was the railway system.

For a start, Australia's worked.

Another was the conductors. In true colonial style, their uniform was smart shirt and jumper, black shoes, long socks . . . and shorts. Quite how anyone can wear shorts and shoes with any credibility I fail to understand, but I guess the Aussie conductors were spared some of the shame due to it being compulsory attire. They did make up for it with an apparent death wish – all of them would ride in and out of stations in the guard's compartment with the door open, hanging out, the wind rushing through their hair and (more often than not) giant beards. They would nod to platform staff, survey the station, and no doubt think 'I may look like a complete Jessie with my shorts and shoes, but at least I get to hang out of trains for a living!'

With British trains' automated doors, plus our health and safety obsession, they'd never get away with that back home.

When I boarded at Sydney, bound for Dapto, I climbed up to the empty upper deck of the carriage (another difference: double-decker trains) and found all the seats facing the wrong direction. All apart from one.

Odd, I thought – carriages usually have some seats facing forwards, and others facing backwards. Mine not to reason why, I thought, as I plonked myself and my backpack down in the one seat facing forwards.

Then other folk gradually came up, and instead of cursing me for grabbing the one forward facing seat, they simply pushed the other seats over, and they swung like upside-down pendulums from backwards to forwards facing.

Reversible seats. Absolute genius.

The two-hour journey south along the coast meandered through dense, dry forests, rolling hills and the large town of Wollongong, and at last with a tingle of excitement we arrived in Dapto.

Well, I had a tingle of excitement – I couldn't speak for my fellow disembarking passengers. They may have had fun awaiting them in Dapto, but none had mullets to look forward to.

I looked around for Lance, the farmer who had emailed me offering accommodation on the back of the newspaper article. When I'd phoned him earlier that morning he said he'd meet me at the station and that I would have no trouble finding him. Right enough, it was such a small station that only a handful of passengers got off, and there was only one person waiting on the platform. It was Lance.

'G'day! You must be Simon!'

It was great to meet him. Not only was he my host for two days, but he was the first person in a week down under to greet me with 'G'day'. Now I'd left Sydney for small town Australia, I felt like I'd actually arrived. I doubted I would see that many cork-rimmed hats but Dapto would surely be a prime place to tick off a few other national clichés.

I instantly took a liking to Lance – he was outgoing, friendly and very down to earth. A tall man with dark hair and a healthy farmer's complexion, I would have put him at around forty, and he was married with two young children. He'd read the article in the Illawarra Mercury following my interview with Dave the journalist, and decided that because I was making the effort to come to one of the less touristy parts of Australia, he'd love to meet me and offer me accommodation on his farm. He told me all this as we drove in his Range

Rover from the station to his farm on the edge of the town.

I explained he was not the only person to respond to the article, and I told him about the postcard collector, the film 'Mullet', and Tanya, the woman who wanted a photo of me with her and her mullet husband.

'Fair dinkum!?' Lance laughed, allowing me to notch another Aussie phrase off my list.

We arrived at Lance's farm, which he explained was partly used for his tree nursery but half of which he rented out to a local community farm collective, meaning with the community volunteers and his own staff, it was a bustling place. The farm building was effectively a large shed, next to which lay a couple of disused railway carriages, one of which was to be my home for a couple of days, and beyond that was the farmland.

Mullet Creek itself ran along the right hand side of the farm, and Lance took me to see it straight away.

'It's not much to look at, I'm afraid,' he said. 'It's covered with weeds and alien trees – mostly English ones. We've done quite a bit of clearing out though so it is better than it was.'

The creek – or stream in British English – was just a few feet across and perhaps barely that in depth. The water looked clear, and the banks on either side were topped with green grass.

I didn't feel it was something worth travelling across the world for, but Lance assured me this was just a small stretch and there was plenty more to see, much of it a great deal prettier.

We doubled back along the creek and Lance showed me to my accommodation. It was an old railway carriage which he had converted into a caravan. There was a large bed, a sofa, a table, and not much more. It was basic, but all I needed for a couple of nights' kip. It wasn't connected to water or electricity, but Lance said there was a bathroom in the farm's warehouse I could use.

Once I'd dumped my bags and settled into my unusual surroundings, I headed into the farm office where Lance was getting some lunch on the go. The building was a simple construction and inside was a clutter of farm machinery in the workshops and paperwork in the office. There he introduced me to some of the other folk on the farm.

Will, a genial man in perhaps his fifties, was the foreman on the farm, and greeted me with a warm handshake. Luke was the 'horticulturalist', which as far as I could see involved not saying very much, wandering around with tools in his hands and listening to the radio on his headphones.

There was also a volunteer, Andrew, who had recently completed a PhD in chemistry and was now filling time on the farm while looking for work. While Lance got some bread and ham out of the office fridge for our lunch, I made the mistake of asking about Andrew's PhD and ended up being confused by huge, sprawling diagrams of molecular compounds.

After a quick bite, however, there was no hanging around – I had arranged to meet Dave Braithwaite from the Illawarra Mercury for his follow-up article.

'G'day Simon,' Dave said as he got out of his car in the farmyard. He was a young guy, not much older than me, and casually dressed. Excellent, another 'G'day'. I rather hoped someone would call me a 'flamin' gallah' before I left town.

'This is Sylvia,' said Dave, introducing his photographer, a blonde woman with a warm smile and handshake.

'So what's the plan?' I said eagerly, while sitting in the back of the car. We were driving along the main highway at the edge of town. It was quite fun having my very own media and chauffeur team.

'We'll go down to the creek, get a couple of photos, and ask you a few more questions for the article,' Dave explained. He sounded quite excited himself; it was probably one of the more off-beat assignments a journalist might be given.

After a short drive, we arrived at a stretch of the creek a little away from town. At last, I thought. Mullet Creek in all its glory. Here I was.

Sadly, like the section Lance had shown me, it was slightly disappointing. It was wider and certainly more scenic, but still just a creek, a stretch of water, a wee river. We stood on the banks of it, in a park. Behind us were a few kiddies' swings and a barbecue, the beginning of a short nature trail, and a few folk fishing just along from us.

As I threw off my shoes and socks and waded into the creek at Dave's suggestion, posing for Sylvia's camera, I felt something of an unlikely celebrity, standing in some very unremarkable water, a couple of old men with their fishing rods wondering what exactly was happening. Actually more than that, I felt a bit of a tube – I was forcing myself to act cheerful in my poses for the camera, more than anything because I didn't want to dampen Dave and Sylvia's own enthusiastic directions.

While I did this, Dave threw a few more questions at me about how it felt (I lied and said it was thrilling to be here at last), and what lay ahead for the mission. Then within minutes, it was all over and we were driving back along the highway.

But as we approached a large road sign, I realised it was the one from Dave's initial newspaper article – we'd swung round on ourselves and were now driving over Mullet Creek. My heart skipped a beat.

'Guys, this is the sign! Can we stop here for a photo?'

'Well, we've got another appointment,' said Sylvia, 'but just for you – seeing as you travelled twelve thousand miles!'

'Brilliant, thank you so much!'

Sylvia pulled the car over, and I scrambled out along the edge of the road to the sign. There it was.

MULLET CREEK
Lake Illawarra Catchment

This was it. I'd finally arrived. The first Australian mullet to be ticked off. The flight across the world, the jetlag . . . it was all worth it for this. The road sign. The proof, the visible evidence that I was here. At Mullet Creek. I reached up to the sign and kissed the warm, dusty metal.

I'd done it.

Meanwhile back at the ranch (I've always wanted to write that), the working day had more or less come to an end, and Dave and Sylvia dropped me off amid my eager thanks.

'Oh, incidentally,' said Dave, as I got out of the car. 'I meant to say – I think there's another mullet for you, in Sydney.'

'What? Where?' I blurted. Another? How had I missed this? And . . . 'incidentally'!? How could another mullet be incidental?

'It's in a place called Narrabeen, on the western edge of Sydney,' Dave said casually through the car window. 'Not sure exactly where it is, but it's called Mullet Creek. Some colleagues mentioned it before I left the office, not sure if you know about it.'

'No! Fantastic! Thank you so much!' I wondered why Dave hadn't told me sooner, but there was nothing I could do about it until I got back to Sydney. Why did his colleagues know about it? Had he got the whole staff at the Mercury searching for more mullets? Were they all keenly following my story?

I didn't have any more time to quiz Dave further, as he and Sylvia had their other story to rush off to. I made a mental note to look up Narrabeen's Mullet Creek, and headed back into the farm building. There was nobody around, so I decided to go exploring.

I walked back across the main road which separated the farm from pretty much the rest of Dapto, and there wasn't much to see immediately – a road stretched ahead of me, presumably towards the town centre, and a turning off to the left passed a row of houses and led up to a church. I took that road.

The church was locked. It was a nice enough looking building, but modern, at least by British standards. I had a peek around the graveyard at the back. It was neat, tidy, and rather lacking in atmosphere. It was almost suspicious, until I realised what was missing: the centuries-old, moss-covered gravestones with faded lettering speaking of quaint names and redundant occupations. Everything here was just so new, even the dead people.

I returned to the creek, recalling the park and barbecue spot I'd seen opposite where Dave and Sylvia had taken me. The park was much as you'd expect, with an installation for barbecues, a playpark, and a toilet cubicle that didn't work. Nearby was a sign for a nature trail that I'd noticed earlier, and I was entertained by the fact that the cartoon character who introduced himself on a large interpretation as the guide on the trail was called Mikey the Mullet. The trail was a pleasant afternoon stroll, with Mikey the Mullet popping up on the occasional signpost to explain a little more about the plants, flowers and fish you could see along the way.

I went back to the main road and headed towards town, passing a service station, a few houses, and a small precinct of shops. I stopped at a pub. My stomach told me it was dinner time, and my throat told me it was beer time.

The Bandaloo was conventionally Australian, as far as I had come to know the Aussie pub. The bar was slightly down at heel, with a few trinkets of rugby memorabilia decorating the walls, and the bar looked well-stocked and unpretentious, designed for no-nonsense drinking. Although there were few folk in the bar (it was still relatively early in the evening) the corner room containing the slot machines was packed. On a wall hung a whiteboard with the results of the weekly pub lottery. I scanned the names of the entrants. Bazza, Niko, Jono, Robbo, and even a Bruce. I was truly in small-town Australia.

I grabbed a table, and ordered a burger and a pint of Toohey's New which I had come to like since arriving in Australia. I was served by a barman who looked like a thin version of one of the bearded ones from ZZ Top.

My food soon arrived and was just what I needed – basic,

substantial and satisfying. I began demolishing it, glad that the simple act of eating gave me something to do to avoid feeling alone and self-conscious.

Yes, some people have nightmares involving going to work with no trousers on, or finding themselves back in school. Mine simply involve being alone in a pub with no mates.

'Thought I'd find you here.'

I looked up. It was Lance.

'Wife and kids have gone to see some friends for the evening, so I decided to see if you were up for watching the footie,' he said, taking a seat at my table. 'You weren't in the caravan so I guessed I'd find you in the nearest bar!'

I had heard one or two people mentioning the big match tonight, and right enough the bar was slowly beginning to busy up. It was the State of Origin, a Rugby League competition where Australians from Queensland and New South Wales would take each other on over three matches. It was one of the highlights of the Australian sporting calendar, and tonight was the decider.

Rugby League (or just 'footie', as they called it here) was not a sport I knew a great deal about. Where I'd grown up, it was just football. Where rugby did have a foothold in Scotland, ostensibly among public school graduates and Borders villagers, it was Rugby Union. Rugby League, however, had its roots in the working class areas of northern England, although it was of course also popular in Australia. I barely understood the rules of Union never mind League, so Lance explained things as the game went. He moved on later to explain Australian Rules football, and how Australia managed to sustain such high levels of participation in so many sports by investing heavily in facilities and encouraging kids to stay involved once they'd left school.

At half-time the best I could do to reciprocate in terms of cultural understanding was give as good an overview as I could of the game of shinty, Scotland's answer to hurling and not dissimilar to a no-holds-barred version of hockey. My knowledge was somewhat patchy though, since it was a game I had never played or even seen other than occasionally on television.

The match finished as a comprehensive win for New South Wales, and was so one-sided that Lance admitted it hadn't been especially entertaining, despite the pleasing result. We departed not long after the match, after ZZ Top the barman had pressed into my hands a NSW Rugby League top and a commemorative DVD of 20 years of State of Origin rugby.

Lance gave me a lift back to the farm, and drove off home. As I walked from the farm building towards my railway carriage, I was briefly captivated by the stars. It was a brilliant, clear night. I looked around and felt quite disorientated – everything was different.

Growing up on Benbecula I'd been keen on stargazing as a child, because the lack of street lighting meant that cloudless nights rendered brilliant, clear astronomical displays, and I had got to know the stars well. Down under, in a different hemisphere, however, the constellations were all totally different. Nothing was familiar. That, more than anything I'd experienced so far in Australia, really hammered home that I was on the other side of the planet.

The lack of cloud cover also meant that, despite the intense sunshine during the day, there was nothing to trap the heat. It was now freezing cold, so I retreated back to the railway carriage and went to bed, one more mullet under my belt, but with a new one to find.

I woke early. The winter dawn was relatively late and the air still cold as the sun streamed through the window. I threw on some clothes, grabbed my towel and hopped out of the carriage towards the farm building to grab a shower.

'Simon!' Will the foreman was at work already and was loading some boxes into a van. 'I have questions for you!' He walked towards the back door of the building to meet me. He had a friendly and enquiring smile on his face.

'Good morning Will, how's it going?'

'Mullets.' He replied. 'So you're travelling around looking for mullets.' I was about to say something before Will spoke again. It clearly had just been a preparatory statement, not an invitation to comment.

'What are your first impressions of Dapto?'I hadn't really seen enough to comment, but didn't want to say that. 'Very nice. Pretty. Quiet, though, but I guess it's out of the way. In a nice way, of course.'

'What are your travel plans after here?' Will asked.

'I'm heading up north, I think. There's another mullet north of Bundaberg, so I guess that's as far as I'll be going.'

'You might see toads,' interjected Will. I wasn't quite sure how to respond to this.

'Right,' was the best I could do.

'Yeah, huge big toads,' he replied, holding his hands a few inches apart in front of him. 'Poisonous things. If a dog ate one, it would die.'

I thought for a moment. Yes, being eaten by a dog would generally have that effect on you. Then I realised he meant the dog.

'Thanks, I'll look out for them.'

'The Chinese are interested in them.' I was really struggling to keep up with Will's idea of how our conversation should develop. I imagined what the Chinese might do with poisonous frogs. Perhaps drop poisonous frog bombs on Taiwan. They would bounce first, presumably.

'For traditional medicine, you know,' he added.

'I see,' I replied, despite the fact that I didn't. How could huge poisonous frogs be good for medicine? Unless of course traditional Chinese medical practitioners were suffering major rat problems of late.

Will then asked me what I meant by a mullet. I explained something of the haircut.

'You know, like Steve Irwin,' I added, giving the most Australian example I could think of.

'Yeah, he's cut his off though,' Will replied.

'So he has . . .' I said. 'Never mind.'

'Enjoy your day,' Will said, suddenly turning around and going back to the van.

My day would be spent mostly in Wollongong, or the Gong as it was known locally. It was the Illawarra region's main city, with a population of around a quarter of a million, and a short commute away by train. From what I read in my Lonely Planet, it didn't really boast a huge amount – a beach, some heavy industry, and that was about it. But I thought it might be good to explore a different bit of Illawarra, and maybe find an internet café to check my email.

Wollongong was a bland sort of place. The beach was lovely, if you ignored the dirty coal-burning factories that formed its backdrop, while the central business district was functional and uninspiring. I bought a pastry and some orange juice for breakfast and a copy of the Illawarra Mercury, and sat down on a park bench to eat and see if Dave's article had gone in.

The front page trumpeted the rugby league victory from the night before, and the other big news, that London had been awarded the 2012 Olympics. I flicked the paper open, and there I was leaping out of Mullet Creek in delight.

Page three. Oh boy. Sylvia's photo looked great, with the trees overhanging the creek in the background, and me jumping up, arms thrown up in contrived glee. In the corner was a world map outlining some of the mullets I'd been to and some I was yet to visit. Crowning it all was the most magnificent headline.

'Mad Scotsman up the creek without a mullet.'

The article itself was short, clinging to the edge of the page which was dominated by my photo. I felt a mixture of pride, delight, and a real sense of achievement. What I'd done, what I was doing, and the mission I hoped to complete one day, was making headlines on the other side of the world. It may have been a crazy quest, and yes Dave was probably right in the headline, I probably *was* a bit mad. But mad enough to get some fantastic responses from the people of Dapto, and mad enough to qualify for page three in the Illawarra Mercury ahead of most of the big national stories of the day.

I celebrated by going to check my email. One message jumped out at me – 'Urgent Message from Amy DeLore, Newcastle journalist', the subject heading roared.

Amy was from ABC, the Australian Broadcasting Corporation, and wanted me on the breakfast show of ABC Newcastle, the regional station of a city an hour or two north of Sydney. She'd seen the article in the Mercury, and wanted to line me up for a telephone interview the next morning. I emailed her back with the farm's number, and went off to explore more of Wollongong.

ELEVEN

The Wondabyne and Narrabeen Mullets

A morning spent ambling around Wollongong was more than enough. It was a pleasant enough city, and further along from the beach the harbour was bustling with fishing boats and tourists, and was overlooked by an impressive lighthouse. Other than that, though, there didn't appear to be much more to see, and in the mid-afternoon I headed back to the railway station to catch a train back to Dapto.

At Wollongong station, I found a call box and phoned Tanya, the woman who'd emailed me about meeting her and her mulleted husband. I had provisionally agreed to see them that night, and needed to make firm arrangements. I called her at work. She sounded absolutely lovely with a bright and bubbly voice. She asked all about my travels.

'Are you still up for tonight?' I asked.

'Of course! I hope you don't think we're a little crazy asking to meet up!' I thought about this. I had absolutely no room to criticise.

'No,' I replied. 'It's no more crazy than what I'm doing!'

I explained where I was staying, and Tanya suggested she and Paul could meet me at the farm, then go for something to eat and do a bit of a spin to see some of the sights, even though it would be dark by then. I said that sounded grand, and I headed into the station to find out when my next train back was.

'When's the next train to Dapto, please?' I asked the cute girl behind the information desk. She *hmmed* and *erred*.

'Aww . . .' she replied with genuine disappointment. 'I think you've missed it.'

I thought about this.

'Never mind,' I said, choosing not to ask her what on earth she meant. 'When's the *next* train to Dapto then, please?'

'Oh, let me check,' she said, looking from her timetable to the screen with confusion on her face. It couldn't be that difficult – Dapto was barely half an hour along the line towards Sydney. I waited patiently. She phoned a colleague and they conferred.

'Quarter past four,' she declared with delight.

It was great to see public servants going above and beyond the call of duty to help customers with their unpredictable, complex enquiries.

So I had a dinner date with Tanya and Paul. Tanya with her outgoing, direct sense of humour and friendliness; Paul with his . . . mullet. Any thought I had that they were anything other than textbook Aussies vanished when they pulled up at the farm in that cliché of rural Australia, a ute, or utility vehicle. They got out to say hello and greeted me with enthusiasm and warm handshakes. We got talking right away as they drove me to a nearby steakhouse they had in mind.

On the way we saw a bit more of Dapto, and I realised that by not having a car and being restricted to whatever I could walk to, I'd missed out on a whole section of town, and Dapto was in fact a lot bigger than I had first thought. And Paul's mullet, I observed from the back of the cab, was indeed a classic. Long, flowing and straight at the back, and cropped short at the sides, front and top. I didn't mention it for now, though. It seemed rude to bring up mullets in polite conversation.

At the restaurant, as we tucked into gigantic and delicious steaks, Tanya repeated the concern she'd expressed on the phone.

'You really must think we're crazies, emailing you and wanting to meet you like this.'

'Well, it's no crazier than crossing the globe to visit a place just because it's got the word . . .' – I uttered the word gingerly – '. . . mullet in its name. It's really nice to meet people, and strangers are always fun to meet!' I explained that I'd done just that in Sydney, staying entirely with people I'd contacted through the travellers' website. They thought it was a great idea so I went on to explain more about the kinds of people I'd hosted in Inverness.

We continued to talk about my travels so far, what I did back in Scotland, and their own lives. They had two young children, who were with a friend for the evening. Tanya did most of the talking; she was as warm and genuine in person as she had been on the phone.

She told me she was an architect, while Paul had a magnificent trade – demolition technician. He destroyed buildings for a living. I was envious: there had never been an option like that when I did work experience at school. It sounded like so much fun.

I tried not to think about Paul's mullet or bring it up in conversation, but eventually decided that I really had to. It was why I was there after all, and I very rarely had the chance to speak to mullets.

'So . . . Paul . . . er . . . your mullet. How long have you had it?' I'd inadvertently spoken with a nervous but concerned tone, as if I was enquiring about a terminal disease.

'Since I was about eighteen.'

'He's always had it, I think,' added Tanya. She was definitely the more chatty one in the relationship. 'The kids want him to get rid of it. They tease him about it all the time.'

'So you don't want to get rid of it?' I asked.

'Nah,' said Paul. 'I work outside lots, so it keeps the hair out of my eyes and the sun off my neck.'

Hang on. Having long hair keeps hair out of your eyes? Surely having no mullet at all would be even better for keeping hair from your eyes? But then I thought about it more. I realised Paul had opened my eyes to the other side of the mullet – I had been coming at it from a completely different perspective.

I viewed a mullet as someone who had grown it, who had over time acquired long hair at the back and kept the rest short. Paul, meanwhile, saw it as someone who had long hair anyway, and had cut the front and sides short. It was like a glass – half empty or half full? I'd always seen mullets as a bit of inappropriate long hair on someone short-haired; but Paul made me see it as some short hair on a long-haired head. At last, I saw the mullet in a different light – a veil (or mullet) had been lifted from my eyes.

It still looked hideous though.

After our meal – which Tanya and Paul generously insisted on shouting – they took me a long way back to the farm, telling me more about the area and showing me the lovely coastline. At least, I'm taking their word about the coastline, as it was pitch black. The area, they explained, had traditionally relied on heavy industries such as coal and steel, but was now seeing a rise in tourism.

I was living proof of that, as the pioneer of the Australian mullet trail.

It had been great fun meeting Tanya and Paul, and staying at Lance's farm. Dapto had been an interesting place, and not only had I visited the mullet but – thanks to Dave the journalist – I had acquired another one to track down back in Sydney.

However, it was time to move on. I'd ticked Dapto's Mullet Creek off the list, and now needed to start heading north. The next morning, Friday, I planned to do my ABC Newcastle radio interview, then bid my fond farewells to Lance and the team, and catch the train back to Sydney, where I would spend the weekend.

That morning, as I sat munching some toast in the farm office, waiting for the phonecall from the radio people, Luke the horticulturalist came in, headphone in ear as usual.

'You heard the news?'

'What news?' I replied.

'Turn the radio on,' he said, with a solemn look on his face and nodding towards a battered stereo in the corner. I did so.

Around fifty people had been killed in a wave of suicide bombings in London buses and underground trains. It seemed the so-called war on terror had come to London in the most horrific and deadly way. For the next hour or two, I listened intently. I thought of my friends in London. I thought of the innocent people caught up in carnage they could not explain or understand. I thought of how people might be reacting back home in Scotland. I listened as news reports came in, Australia's Prime Minister John Howard speaking out in solidarity with a city he said the nation felt closer to than probably any other foreign city, while Australian diplomats in London explained what little they knew.

Of course, mullet interviews were off the agenda that morning. Suddenly, my stupid, pointless project seemed even more stupid and pointless than before.

Over the coming days, I discovered that my friends in London were alright, although many had suffered horrendous afternoons as public transport froze across the city for the day. However, while the bombs had touched the lives of pretty much everyone in the UK (I discovered much later that I had known one victim many years previously, and someone else I knew had lost a distant relative), life seemed to quickly move on in the city, in a manner that the word 'stoic' could have been invented for. I figured that all I could do was get on with what I was doing too.

I got back to Sydney on the train that afternoon, just in time to meet Benj, with whom I would be staying for a couple of nights, and Elaine the Scottish woman who lived with Christine, for a pint. Benj and Elaine were keen to hear all my stories from Dapto, and loved the newspaper article from the Illawarra Mercury I showed them. Benj also said he would look up the mullet in Narrabeen on the internet in the morning. After a drink Benj led us to a comedy club he occasionally frequented, and after a night of conversation and laughter, Elaine headed home and Benj and I headed back to the flat he was house-sitting for some friends who were travelling overseas.

'It's been fun having my own place for a bit,' he said as he drove us back through the streets of Sydney. Drizzle was falling on to the windscreen and the streets were filled with people moving from pub to pub. 'I live with my folks normally, and that's a bit of a crimp on the dating scene.' Benj was actively on the look-out, and had of course left the travellers' gathering when I first arrived in Sydney to go a speed-dating event. I'd always considered that sort of thing to be for people who were either desperate or weird, but Benj was neither. He was an intelligent, professional guy who had travelled extensively throughout the world and just wanted another way of meeting similar people.

'Do you tell women you live at home?' I asked.

'I try not to mention it if I can,' he said. He held his hand to his ear as if in an imaginary phone conversation. ' "Yeah, that's right, I live with my parents, so . . . hello? You still there?" It's not always the best tack to take!'

That night, I slept well. It had been a late night for us both, and Benj's friends' spare bed was exceptionally big and comfortable. As I slept, I had a vivid dream. I dreamt that Benj's friends had monkeys in the back garden.

They called out to me in my dream, their shrieks piercing and loud through the window:

'oooh oooh oooh aaah aaah AAAH AAAH AAAH oo-AAAH-AAAH oo-AAAH AAAH AAAH!!!!'

I woke around nine o'clock, the dream so clear in my mind I couldn't help thinking that it hadn't been a dream, and I really *had* heard monkeys outside. As I struggled to regain full consciousness (always a slow process for me in the mornings) I thought it through logically.

Were monkeys native to Australia? I wasn't entirely sure, but I didn't think so. Even if they were, would it be legal, safe or ethical to keep them in your back garden in a quiet residential area? Surely not. There would be complaints from neighbours. They would fight with dogs (the monkeys, not the neighbours), and lizards or snakes would eat them (the monkeys, not the dogs or neighbours).

No, it must have just been a strange dream.

'oooh oooh oooh oooh aaah aaah aaah AAAH AAAH AAAH oo-oo-AAAH-AAAH oo-oo-AAAH AAAH AAAH AAAH!!!!'

I was wide awake. Bleary-eyed, but unmistakeably in the land of the living, and there they were again! Monkeys . . . in the back garden. Definitely not a dream this time.

This didn't make sense. I crawled out of bed, threw on some clothes, and peered between the curtains. Nothing but trees, the car park, and other houses. I shuffled into the living room, where Benj was sitting on the sofa tapping away on his laptop. I rubbed the sleep from my eyes.

'Benj,' I whined. 'Why do your neighbours have monkeys in the back garden?'

'Monkeys!?'

'Yeah . . . there's monkeys making noises right outside my window.'

'Ah right,' Benj laughed. 'That'll be the kookaburras.'

'Just been looking for that mullet in Narrabeen for you', said Benj, as we ate some breakfast in the living room. 'And guess what?'

'What?'

'There's another one! At a place called Wondabyne, further out from the city, a short train ride away.' 'No way!' He showed me the map he'd found on the internet, and the road atlas his friends had in the flat. Sure enough, on the Hawkesbury River, flowing in from the hills towards Sydney, there was a stretch of water called Mullet Creek, right next to a small, isolated railway station called Wondabyne. It looked something like thirty minutes on the train from where we were in Sydney. Meanwhile the Narrabeen one that Dave the journalist had told me about in Dapto was even easier – just a short drive to another suburb in the west of the city. Benj said he would drive me.

Fantastic. Another two mullets! I'd arrived looking for two, and now I had four. Mercifully, they were within easy grasp. That fun would have to wait, though, since Benj had plans for us that day.

It being a Saturday he was free to show me around some parts of the city that I had not already seen, and he took me on a tour of the Olympic Games sites where Sydney had hosted the greatest show on earth in the year 2000. The games had been declared a great success (as they probably all are), and Benj felt especially attached to the venues because he had worked as an Olympic volunteer during the games. In fact, he showed me the forest of tall pillars outside one of the city's stadiums, on which volunteers' names had been enshrined. He pointed out his name, plus his mother's and a few friends who had also been involved.

Along with Elaine, we were back at that stadium in the evening because Benj had organised tickets for an Australian Rules football match. I'd never seen a game of Aussie Rules, and Benj had invited Elaine along because she too was new to that part of national culture after her recent move from Scotland.

The evening's match was the Sydney Swans versus the Geelong Cats, and it was great fun. I'd never seen Aussie Rules before except once or twice briefly on television, and had an impression of it as a real thug's game, a faster, rougher and more violent version of rugby.

In some senses it was, but I was also impressed by the speed at which the match was played, and the sheer size of the pitch which was well in excess of a football pitch and demanded colossal fitness levels and precisely accurate throws and kicks from the players. Sydney won 105-50, and it was a thoroughly enjoyable game.

I was much more impressed, however, by the fact there were bars in the stadium, and you could buy beer to drink in your seats while watching the game. Something which, sadly, Elaine and I agreed would create utter bedlam should it ever be introduced at Scottish football matches.

The next day, Benj had to go along to the birthday party of a friend's wee daughter, and so while he did that I caught a train to Wondabyne, the station for Mullet Creek on the Hawkesbury River. It was a pleasant journey that took me out of Sydney, beyond the suburbs and through thick forests into beautiful countryside.

I was a bit concerned at what I was letting myself in for, however, because Wondabyne was a request stop only, and from what I could see on the map, there was literally nothing there. Not even a settlement. So why there was a station, I had no idea. But at least I was only going to be there a couple of hours before the next train back – long enough to check out the creek, take the obligatory photo, and then go home again. What was the worst that could happen? Other than perhaps getting eaten by a dingo, of course.

As the train stopped I hopped off the front carriage on to the short platform.

'Don't get lost,' said the conductor, leaning out of the doorway as it pulled off.

'Aye no worries, I'm not going far,' I replied – and as I looked round, I could see I certainly wasn't. There was absolutely nothing there. Though it was certainly beautiful. On one side of the railway line was the creek itself, with a steep, thickly-forested mountainside across the water. On the other side, there was a similar incline, with a sign pointing me towards a hiking trail. There were various destinations, one of which was Newcastle, 165km north of Sydney. I'd probably not manage that in the next couple of hours.

I scouted around the small shelter at the station for evidence of the name Mullet Creek. There was nothing, except the name 'Wondabyne' painted onto a wooden bench. Wondabyne. I said the word out loud to nobody in particular. Wondabyne. It sounded like the sort of cigar a superhero would smoke.

I sauntered down towards the creek itself. Water lapped against the shore. I dipped the toe of one trainer in. Mullet Creek. No mention, but from the map Benj had shown me it was unmistakeably Mullet Creek.

Mullet number four.

I crossed the railway line and climbed a bit of the hillside to get a decent photo, and then came back to notice that at the bottom of the hill not far from the station was a shack, with a sign saying 'quarry' in front of it. The shack was behind an imposing fence and seemed deserted, although there were a few bits of industrial machinery dotted around the grounds. A quarry? Where was the road? And the people working on it? Perhaps it was some sort of ghost-quarry . . . where shadowy, mulletted workers came out only in the dark . . .

Before my imagination got too much the better of me, my return train appeared in the distance. I waved as it approached, just in case the fact that I was standing on the platform was not enough of a hint, and it tooted back and began to slow. I opened a door to board but was surprised by a middle-aged man in a rucksack who got out and walked along the platform.

'Rush hour, eh?' I noted to the guard leaning out of the adjacent carriage.

'Yeah!' he grinned back.

So that was Mullet Creek at Wondabyne. Population: nil. Things to do: nothing, unless you're into hiking or quarrying. But a beautiful spot nonetheless, and a fine place to spend a couple of hours. I was just glad I hadn't travelled round the world only to visit that one.

'So how did you get on?' said Benj as he picked me up at the station.

'Fine. Nothing there, really. Quite uneventful. A bit like the Dapto one to be honest.'

'Great, well let's get Narrabeen ticked off, and see if that's any better.'

It wasn't.

It was literally a creek. A dried up creek, down a side road, on the edge of Sydney. There were a couple of houses nearby, and the road crossed the creek via a short bridge you wouldn't have realised you were crossing from inside the car. Moreover, it took us a while to find our destination, despite my best map-reading efforts. This Mullet Creek did have a sign, though, and signs were of course a good thing. I raised a fist in quiet triumph as we approached it. We got out of the car. I kissed the sign, Benj photographed me next to it, and we went home. That was it.

Three Australian mullets down, and two of those in one day. I was turning into a pro.

TWELVE

Single Adult

That night was my last night in Sydney, and it was a bit of a celebration. Benj was cooking, and Elaine and Christine came round, as did Alicia, one of the others from the website get-together.

I gave a full update on my mullet-hunting, including the day's double mullet successes, and everyone wished me well for the journey northwards. We ate, drank, laughed and talked well into the evening, and Benj's food was excellent. Elaine and Christine had brought a pavlova for dessert, and I was greeted with groans when I asked if this was the cue for dogs to start salivating.

The evening wound up some time after midnight, and with farewells to Elaine, Christine and Alicia and good wishes from them in return, my time in Sydney drew to a close. It had been a great week or so in Australia so far. I'd really enjoyed exploring the city, the trip to Dapto had been an entertaining experience, and I had made some great friends.

But it was time to move on. Onwards, upwards and north-wards. Ultimately, to Mullet Creek, Bundaberg.

My first stop was the city of Newcastle, a couple of hours north up the coast. I'd chosen it for no particular reason – I'd pretty much put my finger in the map and decided that at two hours it was not too long a journey, and looked large enough to boast a good array of hostels to choose from.

After a peaceful train journey I arrived late morning, and checked into a hostel just across the road from the railway station. The hostel's staff were friendly and the rooms basic and clean. Just what I needed. I've always liked hostels: they're rarely luxurious, but you get closer to a random cross-section of humanity than you would get anywhere else, and it's a great way to meet folk you wouldn't otherwise meet.

In this hostel, for instance, I found myself sharing a dorm with a punk rock band. Well, a punk rock band, their manager, and another guy, a dour, unconversant Swede.

The band introduced themselves as Monki Blood, and they certainly looked the part. Bearded, a couple of mullets between them, and the ubiquitous black t-shirts. 'We're sort of punk rock,' one of them explained, 'like early Chilli Peppers'. I didn't show my ignorance by saying the only Red Hot Chilli Peppers song I knew was 'Under the Bridge', and even then I thought it had been a total rip-off of the All-Saints' classic.

Monki Blood included a Mark, a Mike and two Pauls, one nicknamed Eel. They were polite and friendly, moving their musical equipment out of my path and each shaking hands with me as I made my way to the empty bunk in the room. The Swede grunted when I greeted him cheerily.

The band explained that they were from Brisbane, and were on a tour of New South Wales but were stranded for a couple of nights because their van had broken down.

After I had settled in a bit and chatted more to Monki Blood, I went off to see what Newcastle had to offer. It was a small city on the coast, and judging by the harbour it was in that awkward transitional phase between a heavy industrial city with lots of steelworks and shipping, and a trendy seaside town of slick new flats and keen surfers. The seafront was a mess of construction sites and glamorous signs trumpeting the exclusivity of the future builds. Overlooking it all was a tall observation tower from which I could see views out to a few islands, a long peninsula running out into sea, and inland to the drab city centre and up the hill to the cathedral.

I spent the day exploring it all, which was disappointing not just because it was an unremarkable place, but also because it had left me little to do the next day except figure out where I would go the day after. So I, and incidentally the rest of the dorm, including my new rock star friends, got an early night.

The next day was, thankfully, not entirely empty. I needed to do a few things such as buy some reading material (I'd recently got through the Iain Banks I'd brought with me), send some postcards, and figure out my journey north.

The first thing I did after buying a late breakfast was buy the postcards. I went down to the main pedestrianised street in the commercial district which consisted of all the usual clothes, electronics and coffee shops, and found a post office.

'Ten postcard stamps for the UK, please.'

'Oh dear,' said the bubbly middle-aged woman behind the counter. 'Only got ten friends?'

I laughed.

'Actually only five,' I said, 'I'll just write to them all twice.'

'Very good,' she laughed back, 'I wish I could think that fast!'

'Be impressed,' I assured her. 'I'm not normally so fast this early in the morning.' I checked my watch. It was five minutes to noon. Yup, still morning.

After that, I checked out Newcastle's museum, which told the story – among other things – of an earthquake in 1989 that had killed around a dozen people and destroyed many buildings, and the history of the convict colonies in the city. Beyond that, like many of the museums I would visit in Australia, its exploration of the country's history focussed on a number of themes, such as the nation's brutal coming-of-age of during the First World War and the impact of colonisation on the Aboriginal population.

It seemed that two centuries of terrible abuses of the Aborigines had left significant scars on Australian society, and the museums I wandered through on my trip gave me a clear impression that the process of repairing the social and economic divisions between the Aboriginals and Europeans was a difficult and ongoing process for the whole country.

My next job was finding tickets northwards. I'd chosen

Coff's Harbour. I wanted to get to Brisbane relatively soon, and as Coff's Harbour looked as if it was well on the way there, I opted for a seven-hour train journey the next morning that would get me much further north up the coast. It looked interesting from my Lonely Planet, and as it had a vaguely funny name it would do for me.

I bought my rail ticket, hit a supermarket and went back to the hostel's kitchen to cook a bit of food.

Monki Blood came into the kitchen as I was clearing up my mess and they began working together on cooking. It looked like a well-organised routine, no doubt honed over their several days of touring. I went back to the dorm to chill out for a bit, got bored of attempting to engage the Swede in anything like interesting dialogue (he seemed to spend his whole time in the dorm, sleeping or waxing his surfboard), and so decided to go for another walk along the beach. As I passed through the kitchen again, Monki Blood were sitting round a table, chatting to each other and tucking into a very healthy-looking meal of pasta. They all called out 'hello' to me as I went by.

It was only mid-evening, but it being winter it was dark and the streets were quiet. I wandered down to the beach, and took in some fresh air, the waves the only sounds. I was happy just to be still and quiet, even though Newcastle hadn't exactly set the heather on fire in my journey. Quiet until, however, the phenomenon of young folk in cars pitched up and hung around on the promenade, doing absolutely nothing except sitting around, talking and playing loud music.

I smiled to myself. They looked just like the gangs that a mate of mine would often call the 'Nova Crew' in Scotland, thanks to their Vauxhall Novas and other small cars, absurdly decorated with expensive wheel hubs. They all wore baseball caps, jeans slung too low at the waist, and stood around trying not to look uncool by allowing their utter boredom to show. What set these guys aside was the fact that most of them drove not Novas but utes. Ah, the class of Aussie youth.

After I'd people-watched myself to boredom, I went back to the hostel to go to bed. Everyone else was already asleep.

In the morning I got up, packed my stuff, and headed off to catch my train to Coff's Harbour. Newcastle had been a nondescript place. Nothing remarkable to see, not much evidence of a decent nightlife, unattractive buildings, and very little that grabbed me. But the hostel had been just the job, and my fellow residents good company – Monki Blood wished me well on my onward journey as I left. The band had been polite, courteous, well-mannered and friendly; they cooked healthy meals and got early nights. Not even a single tantrum, illicit drug, or TV through the window.

They needed to work a little on their punk rock image, I reckoned.

The next few days passed gently and uneventfully, which for the time being suited me fine.

Coff's Harbour was bland, modern, soulless, and spread out over a huge area which, because I walked everywhere in the bright sunshine, left me knackered. I was alone in my hostel room, and barely spoke to anyone during my time there. So I got plenty sleep, read lots, and watched the world go by from street cafés or on the lovely beach.

My next stop was further north on the Gold Coast. The latter half of the bus journey was in darkness, so I missed the moment that we crossed the border between New South Wales and Queensland. I'd thought about Queensland a lot on my trip. Not just because it was the end of the journey and I would be flying home from its capital, Brisbane, but also because of the girl in the Harlequin pub in Inverness from Queensland from whom I had inherited the daily mullet scoring system.

In a sense the trip was down to her, because if I'd never met her and had that conversation, my enthusiasm for mullet-spotting on a daily basis would never have been so great. For me, she'd turned mullet-spotting from just a mission into an everyday challenge. A science . . . nay, an art, a way of life.

Without her, I might perhaps have pursued the mission less keenly. It was possible I might not even have bothered with Australia.

I stayed in the Gold Coast for a few days with friends of friends whom I had been put in contact with, and I had a pleasant couple of days there, warmed by Queensland's clearer, brighter, stronger sunshine after the greyer, more British weather further south.

The Gold Coast was a busy, overly-commercial city, with tall modern skyscrapers and luxury apartments that ruined the seafront and otherwise beautiful beach, and other than having a nice time with my hosts, the only real highlight was buying a copy of Mullet, the film Illawarra Mercury readers had told me about. I found it on offer in a video store and it was cheap enough for me to decide it would be worth watching.

I was wrong. It was just as vintage postcard collector David's email synopsis had been, and apart from the occasional 'spot the former *Neighbours* star' moment, it was an instantly forgettable film.

By now, I'd spent a pleasant week or so on the road between Sydney and Brisbane, and was looking forward to finishing the long trek. Australia had been good to me, I suppose – the journey north had been disaster-free, relaxing, quiet, and without any stress or hassle. I felt great. But I was also itching for a bit of adventure – solo travelling is no fun. I'd had few conversations, and had eaten mostly fruit from supermarkets and junk food from faceless take-away joints because restaurants are depressing places when you are on your own. More alarmingly, I had rarely been in pubs and really, really wanted to go for a pint with someone.

Travelling is just so different when there's someone else around – someone else's ideas and suggestions to be inspired by, someone else to go out with in the evenings, even just someone else to talk to. But by far and away the biggest advantage of having a travel buddy, as Niall and I had unanimously agreed after our travels round Eastern Europe, was nothing to do with the emotional or intellectual stimulation that company brought. It was simply having someone else to watch your bags in bus or train stations while you went to the loo.

Thankfully, there were a few things Brisbane had in store for me that I knew would liven up the journey a gear or two.

For a start, I would be staying with Noel and Di, the folk from the accommodation website who had stayed with me in Inverness with their daughter Jo, herself still teaching in England. I had been in regular email contact with Noel in recent weeks, mostly him giving me advice about travelling around Queensland. He also explained that Michelle, another of their three daughters, who lived with them, worked for ABC in their Brisbane office and had fixed up an opportunity for me to talk about my mission on their breakfast show. Plus Michelle had put ABC in Bundaberg on to the mullet trail too, so the media interest was hotting up again.

In another happy coincidence, a good friend, Tigger, was going to be in Brisbane just a few days after my arrival. She'd emailed me a while back telling me that she would be in Australia at the same time as me, and she would be spending a couple of days in Brisbane before heading much further up the coast to a friend's wedding. Our Brisbane visits would overlap, so I said I would meet her when she arrived at the airport from London.

Noel met me at a bus stop on the edge of Brisbane – they lived not in the city itself but in a lovely house about half an hour's drive from the city centre. It was great to see Noel again. He looked much as he had the year previously in Inverness, albeit less wrapped up than he had been for the miserable spring weather during their tour of Britain. We chatted non-stop in the car on the way back to the house, catching up on all the latest news and my travels.

Back at the house, Di was away at work but I did meet Michelle, their radio producer daughter.

'Right, Simo, the interview's at 6.50am at the radio studios in town, you up for that?' Australians were often very direct, informal people, and names, items or concepts would have their last syllables replaced with an '-oh' sound wherever possible. Michelle was a sparkly lass, and I liked her style of getting stuck right into a conversation.

'Yeah, I can just about manage that. How will I get in?'

'I'll drive you,' said Noel. Michelle wasn't working the next morning as she was on a late shift that night.

'Are you sure? I don't want to put you out,' I replied.

'No worries,' said Noel. 'I'm an early riser.'

That was kind of Noel, but I didn't want to be dependent on lifts everywhere and be a burden on my hosts. Knowing they lived far out of town I had considered hiring a car for the rest of my time. This would not only make my travels in and around Brisbane easier but it would also give me more flexibility on the trip to Bundaberg and further northwards to Mullet Creek. With Noel's assistance I got some numbers from the telephone book, and phoned round a few car hire companies.

The first one stumped me when they asked how far I would be travelling.

'Oh, er . . . not far, erm . . . certainly not out of Queensland.'

There was a pause on the other end of the line.

'Queensland's a big state, mate,' came the polite but faintly patronising response.

'Oh yeah, so it is. Er . . . well, not much more than Bundaberg and back, then.'

I had to remember I was in the Big Country now.

The rest of the afternoon was spent exploring Brisbane city centre. Michelle headed into work and gave me a lift in her car. She was working late so I would need to get the bus back myself and phone the house to get a lift the last couple of miles as I could not get a hire car until the next day.

The drive into Brisbane took us through sparsely populated countryside and along a busy motorway towards the city, which loomed large in the distance. Brisbane, explained Michelle, was a vast city in terms of area although it had a population of only about a million. It was made up of swathes of low density suburbs, and amongst it all the city centre, modern, gleaming, and bustling, towered up on the banks of the river that meandered through it.

Michelle left me in the heart of the city, and I began to follow my nose. Much like Sydney, it was a clean, modern, commercialised city centre, with any dull 1960s architecture thankfully overshadowed by the sleek tower blocks with their glinting glass and ultra-modern design. Only a few Victorian buildings, such as the city museum and one or two churches, suggested this was a place with any sort of history.

I undertook a cursory exploration of the city, identifying the riverside, Botanic Gardens and one or two other landmarks that would be worth checking out later, then went for a poke around the city museum which stood beside a pedestrianised square. The square was open and paved, and much like urban squares the world over it was dotted with the sort of pointless, formless modern art I've never understood, white collar types eating their lunch, and teenagers falling off skateboards.

The museum itself, for some unknown reason, was filled entirely with Buddhas. Two whole floors of them, in fact. Big Buddhas, small Buddhas, fat Buddhas, smiling Buddhas, Chinese Buddhas, Indian Buddhas, strange-looking, comical and scary Buddhas . . . there were a lot of Buddhas. Either there was some special exhibition on or Brisbane was both the most devout and secretively Buddhist city in the world. Either way, I learned nothing about the city during the hour I killed in there.

Sorry, the hour I *spent* in there. I am sure Buddhists don't approve of killing anything, probably even time.

Soon it was time for me to head back for dinner. Di would be back from work and Lisa, their third and youngest was coming round. Lisa lived in the city and I had actually met her the previous year when she was over visiting Jo in Cambridge a few months after Noel and Di's trip to the UK, and they had done a tour of the Highlands over Christmas and New Year.

I went to the bus station, which hid at the bottom of the vast Myer shopping centre, and after much searching found the right stop for where I was going and joined a queue.

As the bus pulled up it seemed like the queue was moving awfully fast. Nobody seemed to be paying the driver, so I became worried that I should have bought a ticket elsewhere first. I tapped the lass in front of me on the shoulder.

'Excuse me, can you buy tickets on board?'

She turned round, a kindly look on her face. 'Yes, you just buy them from that man standing next to the bus. He's selling tickets,' she added redundantly. 'Are you going to Garden City?'

'No, Eight Mile Plain,' I replied.

'And are you going one way?' What was this, the Spanish Inquisition?

'Yeah, just one way.'

'Then what you need to do,' she said in a motherly way, despite being probably a couple of years younger than me, 'is ask for an adult single to Eight Mile Plain.'

I managed not to be sarcastic back, and instead just thanked her. If it hadn't have been for her assistance, I am sure I would to this day be wandering aimlessly around the Myer bus station, begging for food and sleeping on benches.

I bought my ticket. It had 'SINGLE ADULT' written on it in large font. I wondered whether people in relationships paid a higher or lower fare.

THIRTEEN

The Sensitive New Age Cowpersons

It was a pleasant first evening in Brisbane, catching up with everyone and tucking into some lovely food. In my honour, Di had cooked mullet. It was soft in texture, and plain in taste, perhaps a little like trout. It was my first time eating the fish, and I felt I was being a little more authentic in my search now that I had tasted the food that had named so many of my destinations.

We ended up spending most of the evening going through all the family's Scottish holiday photo albums, and it was strange to be on the other side of the world looking at photos of places which included (literally, in one or two cases) my own back door at home.

Later at night, I hopped on Noel's computer to check my email. Most were from family and friends wanting to know how I was getting on. But one was from the Australian Broadcasting Corporation:

Hi Simon – I manage the ABC Radio station in Bundaberg, and we'd love you to drop in while you're here. We like to think we specialise in eccentrics, and you seem to fit the mould! I had no idea we had a Mullet Creek, so your quest has taught me something. Can you give me a quick call on 07 xxxx xxxx when you get a chance, or email me back?

And how about a phone discussion tomorrow morning on our breakfast program, and we'll ask people to ring in and give you some information? We'd just need to have a phone number to get through to you at 8.40am, and we'd need about 15 minutes of your time.

Let me know what you think, either by email or phone. All the best . . .

Ross Peddlesden.

Brilliant! Ross wanted me not only to pop in when I was further north, but to do an appeal in advance! Michelle or her colleagues from tomorrow's interview in Brisbane had clearly decided to spread the word ahead of my arrival, like a modern day mullet-minded John the Baptist.

I wrote straight back to Ross saying I'd phone early the next morning. His offer of assistance was exactly what I was wanting, and exactly what the Bundaberg News-Mail had failed to offer.

I wrote to the News-Mail again telling them in so many words that their rivals at the ABC were on the case, but they still had a chance if they were quick. For some reason, I felt quite determined I wasn't going to let them ignore me.

My morning was going to be busy – ABC Brisbane in person at 6.50am, and now ABC Bundaberg on the phone at 8.40am. I was becoming a media whore, I thought to myself. Although little did I know just what things would be like in a week or two's time . . .

It was a stupidly early start, before 6am, and it was only getting fully light as Noel – hero of the hour – drove me in for the interview. After a welcome cup of coffee courtesy of the Australian licence-payer (or however ABC is funded), I was shepherded into the studio where I met the breakfast show presenter Tricia, who was alarmingly energetic and excitable for the time of the morning, but then I guess such a bubbly personality is a prerequisite on breakfast radio.

The interview went fairly smoothly, despite the fact I managed to *um, er, you know* and *like* rather too much. At Tricia's prompting I explained the history of my quest, the trip round Eastern Europe, Niall's Mullet League Table, and then the moment I discovered Albania's Mullet on Google.

My host laughed, and a further good sign came in when a caller was put on line to tell me about an old northern Queensland saying, where 'Get a mullet up you' would mean to ask someone to shut up and stop misbehaving.

'That sounds rather painful,' I observed.

Another caller asked if I knew about Mullet Creek on the Hawkesbury River, which yes thank you (and thankfully) I knew about and had already been to.

'Nice work,' said Noel afterwards. He had been listening in the adjacent room. I felt a bit bad turning him into my chauffeur so early in the morning, but at least I would soon have a hire car. First though, it was back to the house for some breakfast, and then my 8.40am appointment with ABC Bundaberg.

Before the Bundaberg interview I nipped online quickly to see what extra attention my website had received as a result of the Brisbane interview. Sure enough, there was one email sitting in my inbox:

Heard you on ABC radio in Brisbane this morning and thought you would like to know about this while you are in the area. It is a channel between two islands just south of the Jumping Pin Bar which is between North & South Stradbroke Islands. You can get close to there by going to Tipplers Resort on South Stradbroke (ferries run from the Gold Coast) and getting one of the boaties at the bar to give you a lift the rest of the way. You had better take your own sign for the photo.

Good luck with your travels

Regards
Dan McCarthy

A fifth mullet! And it was in easy reach! I checked with Noel, and sure enough the Stradbroke Islands weren't too far away. I had been very lucky in that the two extra mullets I'd discovered were within easy grasp, and now Australia's fifth mullet was relatively nearby too, and not on the other side of the country.

I didn't have too much time to think about plans, though, because it was time to talk to Bundaberg.

Wayne, the presenter of my second breakfast show of the day, had one of those classic radio voices – deep, masculine, authoritative, and the sort of tone you would totally trust if they gave you an order or explanation. Perfect, in short, for radio.

'Simon, the first thing I've got to ask is . . . why?' he kicked off while I sat in my hosts' living room, phone glued to my ear. Excellent, a nice open question. And off I ummed, erred, liked, and you knowed, telling Wayne and his listeners the story of how the mission began and how I was getting on with it. I told him about my experiences of mullet-hunting in Dapto and the two in Sydney.

Wayne, however, had a rather disturbing revelation for me.

'I have a feeling that when our surveyors were naming creeks and streams back in the early days, they were not very original, because we were also sent information about a website from the Australian government, their Australian Geoscience website, and Mullet Creek is extraordinarily popular, and by the way,' he added with a sadistic laugh, 'in several states of this country of ours.'

I was silent for a couple of seconds. Maybe more. Certainly it was far too long a silence that one should leave on a breakfast radio show with thousands of listeners. I wanted to swear out loud but I bit my tongue, and all I could manage instead was a rather feeble:

'Oh.'

'So you might have a few to go to,' Wayne continued cheerily (he was clearly enjoying this), 'but that's alright, because you still have, for example, one in the Northern Territory, if you get a chance.'

The Northern Territory? That was the other side of Australia! And that must be at least a hundred miles away . . .

'. . . and there's also the Tiger Mullet Channel, off the Queensland coast.' Aha, I was one step ahead of Wayne on this.

'Yes, I know about that one actually – between the North and South Stradbroke Islands. I'll hopefully be making plans to go there in the next couple of days.'

Not that it would matter of course. The Northern bloody Territory? I'd never get there. The mission was ruined.

However, Wayne continued his mullet talk. He, Ross and the team in Bundaberg had more than the standard interview lined up. Once I'd been interviewed, I was allowed to stay listening on the phone while they put on a song. About mullets.

It was a dreadful country and western song by an Aussie band called, according to Wayne, the Sensitive New Age Cowpersons. Now one thing I can be sure of in life is that I detest country and western music. It's irritating, chirpy, whining and I can't stand it. It's too lively to be classical guitar music, too soft to be rock, and too cheesy to be blues, and thus tragically gets lost between the cushions of the great sofa of musical genres, as far as I am concerned. First they tell me there are countless more mullets to find, then they play me some damn country and western to rub salt into the wound.

That aside, the song seemed to be a passable example of the style, and told the story of a man whose family all had mullets. The chorus was sadly one of the bounciest, catchiest earworms I had heard for a while:

'Daddy wore a mullet, and we all had one too,
It was the only haircut our family ever knew.
Even dear old Mama, and little baby Sue.
Daddy wore a mullet, and we all had one too.'

Dreadful, but compelling. A perfect metaphor for the haircut itself. I was humming the tune for weeks afterwards.

Wayne wasn't finished there, though. Oh no. He had explained to me just before my contribution stopped that the Mullet Creek I was travelling to was named after an eighteenth century settler called Mullett – the creek was spelt, it seemed, with two 't's not one – and Wayne's next guest was none other than his direct descendent, local councillor and citrus farmer Jim Mullett.

Wayne's pre-recorded interview with Jim was an interesting history lesson as much as a thrill of mulletology for me. Jim's ancestor, Edward Mullett, had travelled to the new world opening up in Australia from the village of Strathdon in Aberdeenshire, Scotland. He settled originally near Sydney before heading up to Queensland to farm, and along with a fellow farmer, Walsh, Mr Mullett had toiled hard against much adversity to build up the community and industry in the area around Bundaberg. The two pioneers were immortalised by creeks bearing their names, Mullett Creek and Walsh Creek.

Before I hung up, I was sure to get Jim Mullett's mobile number from the show's production assistant. This man I would have to meet. The production assistant, before he said goodbye, also casually mentioned that the number of mullets they'd found numbered around fifty. I could pick up the list if I popped into their office in Bundaberg.

Fifty. Fifty mullets. It was mid-July and I was back to work in early August. I had limited time, limited money, and seemingly infinite mullets. Well, fifty of them, anyway.

Bugger.

Two radio interviews, a new mullet in the form of the Tiger Mullet Channel, a song, a history lesson, and a man named Mullett. Not a bad morning's mullet-hunting. Apart the fact that there was an unnamed number of other mullets in far-flung corners of Australia, which threatened to put completion of the mission way beyond me.

'What do I do?' I whined to Michelle in the kitchen late that night. The rest of the day had been something of a daze, and I'd done very little, apart from some half-hearted research into Tiger Mullet Channel, and a trip into Brisbane to pick up my hire car. It was a nice little car, elderly, but perfectly functional and easy to drive. I had, however, got spectacularly lost on my way back from the city centre, despite extensive instructions from Noel and a loan of his Queensland road map.

'Well, just visit them all,' she said plainly. We were sitting in the kitchen drinking cups of coffee, shortly after she'd got home from her late shift at the Brisbane ABC office. Noel and Di had gone to bed. 'There's only fifty of them. Internal flights are quite cheap.'

'I can't! I don't have the time. Or money. I've got a job and mortgage to go back to.'

'Well . . . how about just visiting the inhabited mullets?' she suggested.

'Most of the Aussie ones so far have been uninhabited,' I said.

'Okay, so . . . focus on the haircut. Why not just go to the inhabited ones where you could meet a guy with a mullet . . . and . . . um . . . get your photo taken together at the road sign with a mullet fish?' Michelle was trying to be helpful, creative and imaginative. She worked in media, after all.

'Nice idea,' I replied, trying not to sound too depressed or dismissive of her efforts to inspire me. 'But that would mean I'd have to research each place, contact the local media to get help, and it would be hard to get the word around all of them and would require practically my own team of researchers and a major media machine. And I fly home in a couple of weeks. And anyway, there's hardly been any mullet haircuts in the places I've visited so far. Well, only one that I met, at any rate.'

Michelle paused a few seconds and stirred her coffee a bit.

'Fair enough, it's looking bad, but . . . you've still got plenty time left in Australia. Your holiday's not totally ruined.'

It felt like it was, but I didn't say anything. I just went to bed in a foul, foul mood.

*

The next day, my friend Tigger was flying into Brisbane airport, and I got up early and headed off in my hire car to meet her. I knew her through Kieran, and I'd not seen her for a few months, so it was good catching up.

I told her about all the latest highs and lows in my mullet mission. I had made plans to find Tiger Mullet Channel the next day.

'Well,' she said, 'I don't have any particular plans tomorrow – I could come with you.'

I liked that idea – some company on my mullet-hunting would be nice, and despite the fact that I didn't know how I was going to pursue the mission in the longer term after ABC Bundaberg's revelation, I felt I should somehow put up a token effort and do what I could for now. I may not be able to make it to fifty mullets, I figured, but I could at least get to the one that was near me. I'd come all this way, after all.

Tigger's host in Brisbane, a guy named Galen whom she had met in London a couple of years previously, was tied up during the day. So we kept each other entertained for a few hours, exploring Brisbane's two botanic gardens and going for a spin in the hills around the city. Truth be told though, we weren't the best company for each other, as Tigger was fighting jetlag after a sleepless flight, and I was still grumpy after the previous day's cart and horses had been driven through my mission.

At the end of the day, we met up with Galen at his flat. It was a beautiful, spacious flat in a building that had been converted from an old woollen mill, in a very trendy part of the city not far from the river. Galen was a musician and, I was interested to discover, vaguely knew Monki Blood, my friendly-but-not-very-rock-and-roll roomies in Newcastle. We headed out to meet his flatmate, Daneka, whom he was meeting for a drink and some food after work.

Sitting outside in a pizza restaurant, we munched away and all got talking, Galen and Daneka keen to hear about the reason for my trip. Daneka asked lots of questions and was particularly taken with the mullet tour, and her interest was fine by me as I had to confess I was quite taken by her. She was stunningly beautiful, with a dark, Mediterranean complexion. I told her that her name struck me as Croatian, and she said she was in fact a mix of Croatian, Italian and Scottish stock.

She explained that she worked in Brisbane but was leaving to go back home, a town far west into the outback, to work for a few months.

'Then after I've worked and saved lots, I'm off to Paris!'

'Wow, that sounds exciting,' I said.

'Yes, my boyfriend lives there.' Ah well, it was inevitable I suppose. 'Tonight is actually my leaving party in the flat – why don't you come?' I said I would love to, and Galen kindly offered me floor space for the night, which would enable Tigger and me to get an early start the next morning for our day trip to the Stradbroke Islands.

The party was fun.

Galen and Daneka were both arty, musical types, so it was a very cultured gathering in the flat that night. I had some interesting conversations with musicians, painters, designers, and various others of their friends. I sometimes get intimidated around creative types, probably because I am a bit of a philistine in that department.

I'm not musical, and I can't sing, paint or sculpt, but it was genuinely interesting to meet people who were very different from me and whom I would have not normally met. More than that, the talk about Brisbane's apparently rich and diverse art scene presented the opportunity to take my mind off the fact that I was a failure in my own pursuit. The mullet mission had gone down the drain.

Daneka wasn't empathising, however. She still thought the mullet thing was a terrific idea, and in playing the good hostess and introducing me to people, she would refuse to let it rest:

'. . . and this is Simon, from Scotland,' she would say to a friend. And before I could start asking about them, she would tell my new acquaintance with a cheeky and exceptionally cute smile, 'ask Simon about his mullet mission!', and so I would have to trot through my (thanks to ABC radio) well-practised story right up to the moment where I discovered there were fifty bloody mullets Down Under, all to the bemusement of Daneka's friends. I would have got quite irritated with her attempts to keep me talking about the mission, but she was only trying to cheer me up . . . and I might just possibly have mentioned that she was very cute too.

Her quiet optimism was infectious though. Maybe I wouldn't get round the fifty mullets in the next couple of weeks, but I could at least have fun on my trip while it lasted, and succeed in part of my mission – there were two I could still get to, and one of those would be bagged tomorrow in a day trip with Tigger.

The party continued late into the night until some time after 2am. After a few hours' kip on the living room floor, Tigger and I were up and on the go for 8am, and headed off to Tiger Mullet Channel.

Runaway Bay Marina, a pleasant drive south along the coast from Brisbane, was the departure point for the short sail to South Stradbroke Island. We arrived there in plenty of time before our 10am sailing, and decided to get some breakfast at the café there. We sat outside in the glorious morning sunshine and ate, tiredness keeping our conversation to a minimum.

We identified the boat we would be taking. It was run by a company based on South Stradbroke Island, who did tours of the island and had a resort over there. I'd phoned their office a day or two before to book tickets on the boat, and had confirmed with them that it was the best place from which to reach Tiger Mullet Channel. The girl I spoke to was professional and courteous in taking my booking and didn't enquire as to the reasons for my very particular line of questioning, although there was a clear hint of intrigue in her voice.

Our fellow passengers consisted of a handful of families, elderly couples and a large party of loud, energetic Italians, most of whom it seemed were going to be staying over at least a day or two in the resort. As we prepared to board, the Italians leapt around shouting and taking photographs of each other, the boat, each other with the boat, and anything else that either moved or didn't. No wonder, I thought, that it's the Italians who gave us the word *paparazzi*.

The crossing was fast and smooth, and Tigger and I sat in the top level of the boat to get a good view. The water was a beautiful, rich blue, the islands ahead of us appeared to be solid golden beaches and thick green forests, and the sky above was bright and cloudless.

I'd noticed since arriving in Australia, that all the colours seemed big, strong, sharp and unbroken here. In Scotland, the lack of sunshine led normally to muted shades, sometimes feeling as if life was being lived in sepia. No shades of grey in the sky here, though – the country was more a simple patchwork than mixed paints or kaleidoscope.

We arrived in just a few minutes at the pier at South Stradbroke and disembarked. The beach was busy with the busy paraphernalia of beach tourism – jetskis, wetsuits, children with buckets and spades, and the noise of laughter, engines and lapping water. As we got off, resort staff shepherded our fellow passengers into a group to tell them all about the resort facilities.

Tigger and I, however, were interested in one thing – Tiger Mullet Channel – so we broke away and headed to the main resort building. We walked into the reception building and up to the desk.

'You must be the guy looking for Tiger Mullet Channel,' said the woman behind the desk.

'Er . . . yes,' I replied. 'How did you know?'

'Because you're the only ones not to stay back for the lecture about the facilities – you obviously knew what you were over here for!'

'Absolutely, that's me. What's the best way of getting there?'

'You're best asking the staff back on the beach. There's a

guy down there at the boats called Mark, he'll keep you right.'

We headed back to the beach, found him tending to some jetskis, and explained our objective for the day.

'You got two choices, mate,' said Mark, a burly guy with a blunt, serious manner. 'It's either a four kilometre walk to the other end of the island, or I could take you in a speedboat for fifty dollars.'

'What do you reckon, Tigger?' I asked.

'It's your mission,' she replied. 'I really don't mind.' I knew Tigger was just being polite – she still looked tired, from both the party last night and the remains of her jetlag. In any case, I wasn't hugely in love with the idea of a trek across an island I didn't know, to a channel I wouldn't be able to identify by myself. And fifty dollars was just twenty pounds, a price worth paying to bag a mullet.

'Let's take the boat,' I said. 'Then we can have the rest of the afternoon to sit on the beach and chill out.'

'Great idea,' replied Tigger, cheering up at the prospect of an instantly easier day.

So we headed off in Mark's speedboat, bumping and crashing our way across the water at a speed that made me, with my not inconsiderable fear of water, just a little nervous. With the rush of the wind it was too noisy to talk a great deal, but Mark shouted over his shoulder to tell us a little about South Stradbroke Island as we went. The island had a population of about a hundred, pretty much all of whom worked in tourism. He'd grown up on the mainland himself, not too far away. The waterway seemed busy with buoys, pleasure boats, fishing boats, sea birds, and the occasional jetski.

'What sort of fish do they catch round here?' I asked Mark.

'Whiting and flatfish,' he replied. 'And of course mullet.'

'How did the channel get its name? Is there a fish called the tiger mullet?'

'No idea, mate. I haven't a clue,' said Mark, with a hint of indifference in his voice. He clearly thought I was a little odd.

There were islands, small and large, all around us, all

covered in rich green forests, and Mark pointed out North Stradbroke Island not too far away. Tiger Mullet Channel, he explained, effectively divided the two Stradbrokes.

Within a few minutes Mark heaved the boat down to a crawling pace. The water around us lashed and complained.

'Well, here we are – Tiger Mullet Channel,' Mark declared. I looked around. I suppose I hadn't really expected there to be a big marker buoy with a sign saying 'Tiger Mullet Channel Welcomes You – Please Drive Carefully', but I was still disappointed that there wasn't one. Dismissing the faint thought that we were taking Mark's word for it and he could therefore have taken us out to any old stretch of water, I gave Tigger my camera, and she took a photo of me with Tiger Mullet Channel in the background.

I reached over the side of the speedboat and dipped my hands into Mullet number six.

FOURTEEN

From Mullet Channel to Mullet Creek

Back on dry land, I dragged Tigger over to the resort reception, and asked if there were any maps that had Tiger Mullet Channel marked on them. I wanted a bit of evidence, something that said the name on it for my increasing collection of photos, newspaper articles and other miscellany I'd acquired since the mission had begun.

The helpful woman had a rummage around and found a large book for sale that charted the coastal zones of southern Queensland. I flicked through and found the page that had the two Stradbrokes marked, with the Tiger Mullet Channel clearly there. Physical evidence. Not quite a road sign, but the next best thing.

Not being an enthusiast of marine geography, and having no pressing need to identify the shipping routes and fishing zones of southern Queensland, I felt that thirty dollars for this weighty tome was a bit much.

'Would it be OK to get a photocopy of this page, please?' I asked the woman.

'Oh, I don't know,' she said. She called back to a colleague. 'Can we do that?'

They deliberated for a couple of minutes while I reflected on whether the Australian copyright authorities' unannounced raids regularly took in the resort reception of South Stradbroke Island.

'Yeah, alright,' the receptionist eventually said. As she ran it under the photocopier for me, she asked what the intrigue with the channel was.

'I'm trying to visit every place in the world that has the word 'mullet' in its name. This one was number six.'

'Right,' she said, unsure for a moment before laughing out loud.

Evidence obtained, Tigger and I still had a few hours to kill before our afternoon boat back to the mainland. We decided to go and walk over to the east side of the island to sit and relax for a bit. The island was long north to south and thin east to west and so it was only a short walk through a forest to the east coast. The sandy ground was hard going in sandals, but there were a few lizards to be seen, small darts of grey-green which would shoot into undergrowth as soon as we would spot them.

The beach on the east coast was quieter and we had it pretty much to ourselves. I went down to the shore and dipped my feet for the first time ever in the Pacific Ocean. I looked out to sea: nothing but ocean until, presumably, South America.

'Look!' Tigger pointed behind us to the dunes. A wallaby sat there, not too far away from us. I remember someone saying that the island was home to a distinct breed that was found nowhere else. I got out my camera and we both slowly walked towards it.

When we got to about twenty feet from it, it turned its head and calmly hopped a few paces away. We approached a bit more. It hopped a bit further away again. It didn't seem especially scared of us, more irritated. Living on a small island, it was probably quite used to humans. I, however, had never seen one, and was quite excited. It was exactly like a kangaroo, but smaller. We both took some great pictures before it finally got bored of the attention and bounced away over the dunes.

Tigger and I sat on the soft, warm sand, snoozing, munching the food we'd brought with us, writing postcards, and enjoying the peace and quiet. It was a beautifully warm day, and we could see far away to the south the ugly tower blocks of the Gold Coast. It was clear, perfectly warm, and utterly still.

Until it began to rain. Suddenly and heavily. Dark grey

clouds came out of nowhere and spewed rain onto the island, forcing us to retreat under the trees.

By the time we got back to the busier side of the island, the rain had stopped, and so we sat down again on the western beach and chilled out some more, watching the staff and tourists go about their day. An hour or so before our boat back to the mainland, one of the staff whom we'd not seen before came over and started chatting amiably to us while doing various bits and pieces of work on the beach.

His name was Pip, and he had worked on the island for a couple of years. He would be the helmsman on our return sailing. He asked a little about where we came from and what we were up to in Australia. When I said I was from Scotland he said his family had originally come from Montrose, on the east coast of Scotland.

When it came to our crossing back to Runaway Bay, we sat up top just behind Pip at the wheel, and talked some more. He explained that besides working at the resort he also lectured in nautical studies at a local college.

'I've done all sorts of jobs in my lifetime,' he shouted over the noise of the engine. 'This is my fifteenth reinvention.'

'That's more than Doctor Who,' I told him.

'Yeah, well, there's plenty time for more,' he replied. 'I'm fifty-two just now, and still don't know what I'm going to do when I grow up.'

I laughed. I wondered what I would be doing at the age of fifty-two. With the devastating news from the interview with the breakfast show in Bundaberg, I feared I'd still be hunting mullets.

I got back to Brisbane that evening, after dropping Tigger back at Galen and Daneka's place. Tigger was heading north the next morning, to her friend's wedding, then going down to Sydney and Melbourne before returning home to the south of England. I had been very grateful for her company through the day; mullet hunting had so often been a solitary activity. We said our goodbyes, and I drove back to my hosts, doing my now usual routine of getting spectacularly lost on the way.

Michelle cooked dinner and then took me on a night out in Brisbane – she was determined to show me the city's nightlife – and during the evening I updated her on my adventures in pursuit of Tiger Mullet Channel. Brisbane had a lively city centre, with a great range of pubs, and it was a real novelty being able to sit outside in short sleeves, in the middle of winter. Or at least as much of a winter as Queensland could lay on.

It was a very late night, and I had an easy morning the next day, my last one before heading north to Bundaberg.

I spent most of it sitting in the back garden in my sandals, reading and listening to my iPod. Noel and Di's house was beautiful, and such is Australia's plentiful real estate that it was a spacious bungalow with huge grounds. Their front garden would probably have counted as a national park back home. Apart from, delightfully, the occasional wallaby hopping across the far end of the grounds.

There were also some remarkably tame kookaburras which would come close, their heads cocked inquisitively to one side, surveying me. While coaxing one brave wee bird to hop close enough to take bread out of my fingers, I decided that for something that was one of Australia's national icons, kooka-burras were quite ugly creatures. Their heads seemed large and cumbersome compared to the size of their bodies, and their hooked beaks and grey and black feathers made them look not so much sinister as just plain unfortunate.

They did do good monkey impressions, though.

I reflected again on how perfect the weather was, and had been throughout my whole trip. Australians I'd met had often complained about the occasional showers and the cold, but I was absolutely loving it. I suppose humans are an adaptable species, and you get used to whatever climate you live in, and so relatively speaking this was quite miserable weather for them, while I was basking in the moderation. I found it very hot in the early afternoon however, and Di and I could only laugh at each other when I went inside to the kitchen to get a glass of water, t-shirted and perspiring, to find her huddled in a body warmer next to the roaring stove.

It had been great to just chill out doing not very much, but of course I still had one more task before I flew home: Mullet Creek, Bundaberg. The next morning, I packed a couple of days' clothes and headed off up the highway in my car. My plan was to get to Bundaberg, find somewhere to stay for a couple of nights, and spend the next day visiting the creek.

It was about four hours' drive north to Bundaberg along the Pacific Highway, which formed part of the gigantic circular road right round Australia. I felt I was doing a long journey, but in the grander scheme of things, it was just a wee spin for most Aussies. Indeed, that everything was huge in Australia appeared to make even the vastest of distances just one of those things you took in your stride.

It brought to mind a story my friend Mark in Aberdeen told me once about when he had travelled around Australia. Somewhere in the middle of nowhere, he met a guy who was, like Mark, taking a break from a long drive. Mark got talking to him. He was Australian, and it seemed to be just him, his ute, his dog and his backpack. Mark asked what he was doing.

'Driving round Australia.'

'The whole country?' Mark had asked. 'That's quite a feat! How far round have you got?'

'I'm on my seventh circuit,' came the casual response.

I passed various points of interest along my way such as the Sunshine Coast, Steve Irwin's famous crocodile farm Australia Zoo, and lots of pleasant but flat countryside. It was fun to get right out of the city and out on the open road, to give the car a nice run.

Not too far north of Brisbane I passed a sign for the district of Tana Mera, which struck me as a delightful, presumably Aboriginal, placename. My sense of curiosity almost made me turn off and go and investigate, but I didn't. It might have been interesting to explore, however, and I thought idly to myself that I would have had a much easier mission if I had chosen to visit places that shared its name, rather than 'mullet' – after all, there could only be one Tana Mera . . .

Later I passed a road sign that declared 1600km to Cairns, a town much, much further up the coast from Bundaberg. One thousand, six hundred kilometres. I shook my head with disbelief – the biggest distance you would ever see marked on a British road sign would be about a hundred miles or so. If I'd left Inverness and driven 1600km, I'd take in about half a dozen countries, hear the same number of languages, and cross at least one timezone, not to mention the English Channel. Here, I could have done the same distance within the one state. Albeit perhaps with the occasional toilet stop.

I had a good day's drive, with a couple of stops at soulless service stations to stretch my legs. Driving in Australia was easy: roads were straight and empty; radio stations I picked up were good company; and that the country drove on the left meant there was no adjustment from driving at home.

It was a refreshing change from being on foot, too – while walking around in Australia, I often had to consciously remind myself that just because I was abroad, didn't mean that the traffic was the wrong way round. The UK is one of the few left-hand drive countries in the world, and when we go abroad it is quite often to mainland Europe or North America, where they drive on the other side.

In Kosovo in 1999, I'd almost been hit by a car when I'd stepped into a busy road having instinctively looked the way I would had I done at home. The screeching of brakes was the first indication that all was not well and although I had time to jump back I had the driver's quick reactions to thank for avoiding what could have been a nasty bump. When he quickly got out and started shouting, I wasn't sure whether it was anger, shock or concern for me, so I just gestured to him that I was okay but apologetic, and got away as quickly as I could.

Ever since then, I've been extra-careful on foreign roads to look the other way, and since coming to Australia, a foreign country that often felt more North American than British, my instincts had struggled to let me simply relax and treat the roads as I would back home.

As the afternoon pressed on, flat farmland, fields of crops, and signs advertising Bundaberg's famous rum signalled to me that I was approaching my destination. Bundaberg was a small but spread-out town, and once I reached the bland town centre I parked my car and went off hostel-hunting. There was one that grabbed me from the Lonely Planet, just a short walk from the centre, but they were full up and directed me to another, across the road and next to the bus station, where they were thankfully able to take me in.

I moved the car to the hostel car park, and settled in. It was perfectly adequate and functional. I had a comfy bed in a clean, windowless room with no other occupied beds, and the hostel also boasted a spacious kitchen and TV lounge. It seemed quiet, though, and there were few other guests. Quite how across the road was full and here was virtually empty, I wasn't sure. I wondered if there was something everyone else knew about this hostel that I didn't.

It seemed, however, to be connected to, or run by, a diving tours company, judging by the adverts and diving gear store-rooms next to the hostel building itself. Prominent signs in what I thought was Japanese also suggested the importance of that market to the tourist economy in this part of the world.

As I walked into the town centre, I noticed the offices of the elusive Bundaberg News-Mail which were, by handy coincidence, just a block or two along from my hostel. It was still just about office hours, so I decided to pop in and see if I could talk to anyone. The last time I had contacted the News-Mail I'd tried a different tack, emailing Brad Petersen, their chief of staff. He was not much more helpful than Lucy Ardern the editor in her initial email – Brad simply told me (using at least three spelling mistakes) that they would be interested and I should keep him posted about when I would be coming, and they'd arrange to have a journalist available. I responded immediately with my intended date, but had heard nothing back since then.

'Hello,' I said at the office reception. 'Is Brad Petersen available by any chance, please?'

'I'll check,' said the woman at the desk. 'What's your name?'

'Simon Varwell.'

'And where are you from?'

'Scotland.'

'I thought that was a Scottish accent,' she said. 'And what's your visit concerning?'

'Mullets,' I replied. A pause.

'Mullets?'

'Mullets,' I confirmed.

'The fish or the haircut?' she asked, a look of confusion on her face.

'The haircut. Well, and the placename.'

'Hold on, and I'll check if he's available.'

Brad came out to speak to me briefly. A slick, thirty-something guy in a crisply-ironed shirt, he smiled a professional smile and said he'd get someone to come and meet me.

I sat down and flicked briefly through the day's issue of the News-Mail, and after a few minutes a smartly-dressed young female journalist came over and directed me to a meeting room, where we both sat down. She introduced herself as Megan, but pronounced it, unusually, with a long 'e'. I was dying to ask her if she avoided meat or dairy products in her diet as then she could be known as Megan the Vegan, but I decided it might be somewhat rude to make such an enquiry at this early stage in our conversation.

I explained a little about the purpose of my visit. She'd not heard of it, or of Mullett Creek, and Brad had mentioned nothing about the mission to her. I might have rolled my eyes with exasperation at this point, and if I had I hoped she didn't notice. So I started from the beginning, telling her the full story of the search. Megan took extensive notes in shorthand, stopping me here and there to ask questions.

When my story reached Australia I told her about the media interest, explaining how I wasn't really interested in it for the attention after the visit, but the constructive advice from readers and listeners beforehand. I told her how helpful Dave Braithwaite at the Illawarra Mercury had been by doing a public appeal for information in advance of my visit to Dapto.

'Ah, bit late for that, really,' Megan conceded.

'Yes, well . . . I did email ages ago, and I also did an interview with ABC Bundaberg too, who put out an appeal for me and were really helpful.' I figured there was no harm playing the local media off against each other. 'They even arranged an interview with the local councillor, Jim Mullett.' Megan raised her eyebrows in surprise, suggesting she knew the name.

'So when are you off to Mullett Creek?' she asked.

'Tomorrow – probably in the morning.'

'Well, we couldn't get anything in the paper until Wednesday or Thursday,' Megan said. 'We wouldn't manage an appeal, but it would be better than nothing.'

What a great tagline for their efficient, eagle-eyed journalism that would be, I thought: *The Bundaberg News-Mail – Better Than Nothing.*

'Are you taking photos as you go?'

'Yes,' I said, giving her my website address.

'Can you come back tomorrow after your visit to the creek with a photo?' Megan asked.

Now they were really plumbing the depths. First *I* have to chase *them* with the story, then *they* ask *me* to do the job of a professional press photographer. What was wrong with the media in this town? The News-Mail needed spoon-feeding, while the guys at ABC had pretty much ruined the mission by finding me fifty extra mullets. Two extremes – lazy lack of interest on the one hand, and enthusiastic overkill on the other. Honestly.

I left the News-Mail office with Megan's contact details

scribbled on a sheet of her notepad (no business cards here), feeling frustrated with the meeting. Megan was lovely and had done her best to be helpful, but her superiors had hardly been quick off the block. It wasn't that I was desperate for the media coverage, for although the Illawarra Mercury's headlines had been exciting to read, that wasn't the point. The point was just visiting the mullets, and only using the local media to get help along the way if I needed it.

To be honest, then, I didn't really mind that the News-Mail were slow on the uptake – it just mildly narked me that they had failed to offer the chance for an appeal for information about the creek before my arrival, missing what experience elsewhere in Australia had suggested was a sure-fire source of assistance and advice about the local area.

Ah well, I figured, it at least looked like there might be some sort of article in the next day or two, and that was, in Megan's own words, 'better than nothing'.

After that, I found a nearby internet café and spent an hour or two catching up on emails, which was a frustrating experience because the woman behind the desk was looking after a constantly screaming baby in between dealing with customers. It wasn't just crying, it was shrieking, wailing and screaming its eyes out. It hit the occasional piercing note that was so blistering it made me and my fellow customers stop typing, wince in pain, and fear for the integrity of the windows and computer screens, until the baby eventually dropped back from the brink by a couple of decibels.

By the time I was done there darkness had descended, but nevertheless I decided to head off on foot to explore more of Bundaberg.

I'd love to give you a detailed, cultured and 'just reading it makes me feel like I'm there' literary exploration of the town, but to be honest it wouldn't be worth it, even if I had the wordsmithery. Bundaberg was just a sleepy-looking, well-ordered place, with neatly-lined streets in the central business district, all the usual shops, the occasional unwelcoming-looking pub, and single or double storey buildings built in either the late nineteenth-century pioneer style or the unimaginative 1960s box style.

I've never understood why the 1960s gave us such a horrendous architectural legacy by way of the brutalist, lumps-of-concrete theory of design.

In other senses, that decade is famous for its hedonistic, 'flower power' culture when British people, a generation after World War Two, let their collective hair down, rebelled against war, authority and anything else it felt like targeting, and gave us spaced-out thinking and drugged-up music. The swinging sixties still resonates in today's popular culture, and while I would not want to be accused of condoning drugs it's undeniable that many people believe that drugs made that era what it was. It is argued that the mind-altering substances helped make the decade's art so flamboyant, radical and beautiful. Where, many folk ask, would the Beatles, Woodstock, the beat poets, Jackson Pollock, or all their contemporaries, have been without the psychedelic influence of illicit drugs?

My question, on the other hand, is if the drugs were that good for the poets, musicians and designers, how come nobody invited the architects to the same parties?

My pedestrian survey of the town centre took me through a couple of moderately pleasant parks, along the river for a bit, and back in along the main road. I didn't see too much or venture far, as it was dark and I wanted an early night. It was, after all, my last day of Australian mullet-hunting tomorrow, and I wanted to be in tip-top shape.

The next morning I slept in, no fellow backpackers to disturb me, and no window to allow sunlight in to wake me. After a shower, I felt fresh, energetic and ready to hit the road.

Noel's roadmap showed Mullet Creek to be about forty kilometres north of Bundaberg, and it appeared to have a railway station – or at least that's what I assumed the small black rectangle on the railway line indicated on the map. Before I left, though, I wanted to see what the tourist information office on the main street had to say. I'd emailed them before leaving for Australia, of course, but they'd helped me only in terms of identifying the precise location, offering me nothing about the history or environment of the place. Now there was hopefully a file of at least one enquiry about it, I wanted to go and see if they had responded to the infinity percent increase in demand and were any better informed now.

I went through the tourist centre's door. It was an attractively-laid out space, with tables of information, posters and adverts with details of tours, hotels and travel information, and a neat reception desk at the back. Two people, an older woman and a bald, middle aged man, were shuffling around the room putting meticulous effort into straightening leaflets on the tables. Another woman was staffing the reception desk. I seemed to be the only visitor.

The man asked me what he could do to help, and I explained that I was looking for information about Mullett Creek. He ummed and ahed for a bit.

'Hilda might know . . . Hilda?' he called to the woman at the desk. Hilda came over to help and the man repeated my query to her. She led me over to a rack of brochures, saying she had a feeling it was mentioned in one particular leaflet, but on inspection found it wasn't. Hilda asked why I was interested, and I told her.

'Didn't you email a few months ago?'

'Yes, that's right.' I said.

'I replied to that,' she said.

'Yes,' I replied, deciding not to remind her that she'd not really helped me in any way. Well, to be fair she'd told me exactly where it was, without being able to tell me anything about the name or history. And that was fair enough, I figured. They were tourist information not a local history centre, and ABC Bundaberg had gone above and beyond the call of duty on the local history front.

In the absence of any other knowledge from Hilda or the leaflet-straighteners, I thanked them for their help, and headed off. The only way to find out anything more about Mullett Creek now, I reasoned, was simply to go and visit it myself. I hopped in the car and headed a few minutes' drive out of town and along the quiet road, lined on either side by dense scrubland.

When I saw the sign approaching, I pulled over next to it by the side of the road.

Mullett Creek.

Two 't's – presumably the first one I'd been to down under that was named not after a fish, but a person. A Scotsman, no less. I looked up and down the road. Nothing. No traffic. No sound. No applauding crowds congratulating me on my achievement, my fifth and final Aussie mullet and my seventh in total.

On scouting around, I noticed that further down the road there was a clearing, where a sign said 'Mullet Creek: Frontage Land Sale'. Besides noticing that they'd spelt 'Mullet' with only one 't', I wondered if there was a property boom. The clearing was occupied by just one house. It looked empty. There was no car outside, no barking dog, no sign of life at all. It appeared abandoned or just recently built. Maybe, I figured, if I came back in a few years this would be a bustling metropolis. Certainly if I'd known anything about real estate, I would have been tempted to make enquiries about a purchase myself.

Just across the road there was another turn off, through a gap in the trees. I followed it to a railway line. The road (actually more of a track) crossed over the railway at a level crossing and disappeared into the trees. So that was it – not a station, just a level crossing.

That was the sum of Mullett Creek as a centre of communications.

I scrambled down from the road to the creek itself. It was dry and overgrown with ugly, thorny bush. Queensland had been suffering severe droughts in recent months, and I imagined the creek had been dry since the summer. Not a drop was left. I clambered back up and took a couple of photos, then hauled myself up to kiss the sign. I'd done it.

I didn't feel anything, though. No joy, no elation, no relief, no jumping up and down with tears of unbridled delight. I just felt like a man standing next to a road sign.

I got back in the car and drove back to Bundaberg.

FIFTEEN

Business at the Front and Party at the Back

It wasn't even eleven o'clock in the morning by the time I returned. I had a whole day and night to kill. I wanted, however, to meet up with Jim Mullett, descendant of the man who gave the creek its name, and whose telephone number ABC Bundaberg had given me when I was on the phone for the radio interview. I called Jim from a payphone, and got him on his mobile. He'd been expecting to hear from me, and after a brief and pleasant chat he suggested we met up in an hour or two for lunch.

That gave me a chance to catch up on my email and burn some photos from my camera, which was now full again, on to a CD. I returned to the now thankfully peaceful Screaming Baby Internet Café and met Jim right outside it later on.

Jim was probably about fifty, a big man with a strong handshake and laid back manner. He took me to a Chinese restaurant and we instantly got stuck into two of my favourite pastimes, talking and eating. Jim, besides being a local councillor and citrus farmer by trade, was a family history enthusiast, and he told me what he knew of the Mullett family. I'd heard a lot of what he had to say in the radio interview, but I appreciated the chance to hear it in person and ask him further about it.

Mullett and Walsh, Jim explained, was a well-known partnership in the world of business in mid-nineteenth century Queensland. Walsh was a minister in the Queensland government, and he and Edward Mullett, Jim's ancestor, had worked hard to develop large-scale agriculture in the area. Jim had investigated as best he could, but information on the Mulletts was scant, and he sadly had no idea if his ancestor had brothers and sisters. He did, however, find record of a small handful of Mulletts from Edward's home area in Aberdeenshire among the First World War's casualties.

Jim had even been over to Scotland a few years back to pursue his research, and asked about where I came from. When I mentioned I lived in Inverness he said he had been there, and had briefly put his local councillor hat on to pay a visit to the Town House.

'The only place outside Downing Street to have hosted a meeting of the British Cabinet,' I interjected.

'That's the first thing the Provost of Inverness said to me,' laughed Jim.

'Yeah, it's one of the facts just about every Invernessian knows,' I said. Back in 1921, a crisis had broken out in Ireland and David Lloyd George, the British Prime Minister, wanted to convene an emergency meeting of his Cabinet. It was summer, though, and Lloyd George was holidaying in the Highlands, so rather than travel back to London he called the Cabinet up to Inverness to meet in the council chambers in the Town House.

Other claims folk have made about the city are that it is or was the fastest growing city in Europe, the Proclaimers were discovered there, and a cinema on a retail park to the east of the city was the first cinema in the UK to have both digital sound and vision.

I didn't bore Jim with an Inverness factathon, however, and instead asked more about his work.

Jim divided his time between local government and citrus farming. He owned a vast farm that sounded bigger than some European principalities, employed numerous staff, and his family were all involved in the farm too in various respects.

Besides that, he told me, a big love of his was flying. He owned a small plane, had numerous friends who also flew, and would regularly head off across Australia with them. He said it was great fun, and seeing the country from above, especially the desert, was just beautiful. I could only imagine.

'In fact,' he said as our lunch drew to a close, 'I'm keeping half an eye on the clock because I've got to fly to Maryborough, a town near here, to get a couple of minor repairs done on the plane. I need to be there and back before it's dark.' So we wound up our fascinating conversation and left the restaurant, Jim refusing to let me pay for lunch.

Outside, as we were just about to shake hands and part company, Jim's mobile rang.

'Yes . . .? Yes, he's with me now. What, just now? Well, time's a little short, I've got to . . . well . . . yes . . . yes . . . okay, fair enough, we'll be there in a minute.' He hung up. 'That was the News-Mail, they want a photo of us at Mullett Creek!'

Jim and I sat in the same meeting room Megan had interviewed me in the day before. Megan came in.

'Sorry guys, we're having trouble finding a photographer,' she said with a forlorn expression. 'Our usual one is off with toothache.' It seemed the paper was down to its usual standards of organisation. With Jim getting a little agitated about missing the daylight for his flight to Maryborough, the back-up photographer Tanya eventually appeared and the four of us headed off in one of the News-Mail's cars for the creek, while Jim filled Megan in on his connection to the story.

We arrived at Mullett Creek, the scorching afternoon sunshine beating down on us. It was funny being back again. This would be the first of the mullets I'd made a return visit to. It was much the same, still deserted. Tanya assembled her very professional-looking camera, and began casing out the area around the road sign to get the best shot of it with Jim and I. She directed us into various poses: beside the sign, far in front of it with it in the background, and moved us around to best avoid the direct sunlight. It was like being some sort of film star or model, having to maintain a smile which was becoming more and more fake and forced as we went on.

Tanya even suggested we try an unusual shot with Jim in the foreground and me halfway up the tall road sign at the back of the shot. I clambered up as best I could, and the sign swayed by an inch or two.

'Sorry to have you complicit in damage to council property, Jim,' I said.

'No worries,' he smiled, waving his hand dismissively, 'different shire.'

Tanya eventually settled on a good shot, just before Jim's depleting flying time and my low heat tolerance led us both to lose our tempers. The shot had me in the foreground, Jim in the background, and us both turning back to point at the sign. The meticulous professional satisfied, the four of us drove back at top speed, quickly dropping Jim off at his car so he could drive to his airstrip.

I'd been rather tempted to ask Jim if I could come with him on the flight, but I had agreed to pop in that afternoon to the ABC Bundaberg offices to say hello.

Ross Peddlesden, the station manager, who first emailed me about the interview I did on the breakfast show, was the only member of staff in the office.

'The local stations don't do all their own shows,' he explained in a deep, soft and warm voice that you could imagine presenting a late night jazz show. He poured himself a coffee. I'd declined his offer of a cup, and instead parked myself next to the water cooler and began knocking back shots of its icy-cool contents.

'We do a lot of our own stuff, such as the breakfast show, the news and the like, but switch over to national stuff later on,' he said. 'So the afternoon is quiet for us.'

We sat in the office and he told me a little more about the research behind the interview Wayne had done with me on the breakfast show. Jim Mullett was well-known locally, and they were in touch with him most weeks to get his views on local issues. I said the country and western song had been a novel touch, although I didn't tell Ross I hated the genre with a vengeance.

'Yeah, the Sensitive New Age Cowpersons come from Perth in Western Australia, and they're one of the best country and bluegrass bands in Australia. They spend most of their time touring and do a lot over here on the east coast.'

Ross asked more about the rest of the mission. He was interested to hear about my adventures back down the coast in Dapto.

'The Illawarra area's famous for two things,' he said. 'The Dapto Dogs racing circuit, and the Auntie Jack Show.' He explained that The Auntie Jack show was a comedy show in the 1970s set in Illawarra, and which was not dissimilar to Monty Python's Flying Circus. From now, I suggested, it would be famous for mullets too. I told him about the media interest down there in the Mercury.

'That reminds me,' Ross said, getting up and walking to a messy-looking desk. 'That list of the fifty mullets from the interview . . . I must get that for you.' I sighed. He had to remind me, didn't he? He shuffled a few papers.

'It's somewhere here on Wayne's desk . . . he's not in because he works so early. He leaves his desk in such a mess. It must be here somewhere . . .' Eventually Ross appeared to give up. 'Well, no idea where it's gone,' he said, sounding disappointed. 'And if you don't have the list, how are you going to know they exist?'

I thought for a second. Of course! How indeed? I'd been obsessing about the fact that I had fifty more mullets to find, and yet I was taking the ABC guys' word for it that they existed. If I didn't have the list, the evidence of the locations, then they surely weren't mullets that I had to visit. After all, I could only visit the ones I knew about. These were ones I didn't know about – their names, locations, how many there were, anything.

This was my escape clause! This was me back on track!

'Oh don't worry, Ross,' I told him. 'Don't waste your time looking. It doesn't matter.' 'Well, I could have another look . . . and maybe when Wayne's in tomorrow I could get him to find it and send it to you?'

'Honestly,' I insisted politely, 'It's no problem. Really don't worry about it.'

Realising that I needed to let Ross get on with some proper work, and fearing he might suddenly remember where the list was and hand it over, I made my excuses, thanked him for all his help, and asked him to thank Wayne and the rest of the team for their efforts. Despite the fifty extra mullets, it had been a fun interview with ABC Bundaberg, I'd learned a lot, and it had put me on to Jim Mullett.

I left the ABC offices, and scrubbed off my mental list some fifty mullets for which I had no evidence. I was back in business.

Despite my desire to celebrate the resurgence of my mission, I ended up spending part of the night going to an internet café for about an hour then reading in the hostel. The town centre was dead. I stuck my head round the door of a couple of pubs only to find them utterly lifeless. The nightlife of small towns on Tuesdays was not exactly party central. Something of an anticlimactic end to a couple of very good days in Bundaberg.

In the one pub where I did find a bit of life, I parked myself at the bar and ordered a drink. There were a handful of backpacker types sitting around a few tables, and some older guys, I guessed locals, playing pool in the corner. Before long, a quiet chap next to me struck up conversation. He was, judging by his skin colour, Aboriginal. In a friendly but slightly awkward manner, he asked a little about where I was from, where my travels were taking me and my perceptions of Australia.

After a few minutes, however, a drunk, obnoxious woman marched up to us and began interrogating me loudly and incoherently. A few heads around the bar turned towards us in annoyance. My new acquaintance introduced her, somewhat apologetically, as his sister. Quickly, she became more slurred and started getting aggressive towards me, him, and the room in general. Her embarrassed brother reluctantly gave up trying to cope with both talking to me and containing her behaviour. He said sorry, bade me goodnight and dragged her off out of the pub.

Although I'd learned a fair bit about Aboriginal society from a couple of museums along my route, I'd wished I could have talked longer to the guy. All the other Aussies I'd met in my six-week journey had been white, and Aboriginal life was something I'd not really had a chance to hear about from anyone directly. In fact, other than the musician I'd seen playing the didgeridoo in Sydney on my very first day, the only other Aborigines I'd seen since arriving in Australia had been either drunk in parks or homeless on the streets.

The next morning I decided to head off early. I would be driving back south, to the city of Toowoomba, about an hour or so inland from Brisbane, where I would be staying for a couple of nights with some friends of Noel and Di, giving me a chance to see a different part of Queensland. After checking out of the hostel I threw my bag in the car and headed to the main street with the intention of buying a paper and reading it over breakfast.

I picked up a copy of the News-Mail in a store, and unfolded it.

Streuth, as the Aussies would say.

I was only the front page headline.

'Man's Mullet Mania'

. . . declared the News-Mail, underneath a giant picture of myself and Jim next to the Mullett Creek roadsign. I bought a copy, settled down outside the nearest café with a coffee and pastry, and read the article.

Scotsman Simon Varwell's worldwide 'mullet' mission is just like the infamous haircut – business at the front and party at the back.

Mr Varwell's 'business' or unusual obsession with the haircut, sees him travelling the world in search of towns with the the word 'mullet' in their name.

His personal studies in 'mulletology' have brought him to Bundaberg to visit Mullett Creek just north of the city and to meet local citrus grower Jim Mullett.

The creek was named after Mr Mullett's ancestors, so this well-known local had plenty to tell the inquisitive foreigner.

Mr Varwell's interesting quest started a few years ago.

'I like to see how many mullet haircuts there are to see if there is any correlation between the name of the place and the hairstyles,' he said.

He will leave Australia today on the search for more 'mullet' towns.

– MEGAN CUNEEN

Nice work Megan, I thought, despite the fact I was just leaving Bundie, rather than the entire country, today. I also couldn't help noticing that Megan had referred to my 'interesting quest'. It seemed an odd adjective to describe the mission. 'Interesting' was one of those bland words that people sometimes used when they actually meant 'completely bonkers'.

It was a neat article, though, and a great photo. It was just slightly ironic that over the months I'd been chasing the News-Mail up, they'd not once taken an interest, and now I'd arrived and hassled them they'd made it front page news.

Was my visit really the region's biggest story of the day? Probably not, but I wasn't complaining. In fact, I was grinning a rather big-headed grin, and I must have looked very vain sitting outside a café reading an article about myself. I hoped that nobody noticed me.

The next few days were quiet and relaxing.

I had a gentle drive back down the coast and through the hinterland to Toowoomba, where I spent a couple of nights with Noel and Di's friends. They were great company and kind hosts, and the town itself was very pleasant, set amidst some beautiful countryside, lovely views of which could be gained from the treeless landmark Tabletop Mountain.

When I returned to Brisbane I had just enough time to return my hire car and then head straight off again with Noel and Di to the Sunshine Coast, a pleasant strip of coastline not far from the city that was bustling with tourists but avoided anything like the rampant, soulless commercialism of the Gold Coast.

Noel and Di were, in league with various other friends, house-sitting for some people who were away on holiday, and decided it would be a chance for a short break. I was invited along and spent a couple of days doing absolutely nothing except reading, sleeping, eating and sitting on the beach watching the world go by.

Getting back to Brisbane just a day or two before I was due to fly back to London, I felt I'd really been on a relaxing holiday. Those last few days since Bundaberg, with the mullet-hunting out of the way, had been peaceful and uneventful, and I had enjoyed the chance to recharge, be as lazy as possible, and take a deep breath of satisfaction at the end of the Australian leg of my mission.

The trip had been an unparalleled success, I reflected while ambling along the beach one afternoon. Sure, there'd been some highs and lows, but overall it was a success. I'd come out looking for two mullets, but ended up finding five, doing a few radio interviews, appearing in two newspapers, and having a great time exploring a beautiful part of the world. Mission more than accomplished.

As the three of us drove back from the Sunshine Coast, though, I switched on my phone to check for any text messages from home. I had just one. It was from Lance, my host in Dapto.

Back page of the Sydney Morning Herald last Thursday – you media whore, you!

What!? The Sydney Morning Herald? They were one of Australia's biggest newspapers! I'd not spoken to them. They must have picked up on the article from Bundaberg and done a story themselves. Yet more media interest – and this time, national!

However, when we got back to Brisbane and I caught up with my emails for the first time in four or five days, I realised that it wasn't just the Sydney Morning Herald that was on to the story. It seemed the News-Mail article had created something very close to a nationwide media frenzy . . .

My inbox was groaning with requests for interviews from radio producers and newspaper journalists from across Australia – including ABC stations in Perth, Melbourne and the Gold Coast, commercial radio in Canberra, and two nationwide ABC stations, Radio National and Triple J. Plus a TV station wanted me for a regional show going out over most of Queensland.

When I returned to Scotland just under a week later I found that one journalist had even attempted to track me down via work, which left our press relations guy somewhat taken aback because he – and most of the rest of my colleagues – knew nothing about the mission.

I gulped. This was the big time.

Over the next day or two, Noel and Di's house was turned into something resembling a media centre, with me hogging the phone line to do radio interviews and keeping track of the emails as they came in. The interviews were a mix of live and pre-records, but they all seemed to be breakfast shows for some reason.

I wasn't sure why mullets were more suited to breakfast than any other time of day. I wasn't entirely chuffed about the very early starts I had and to be honest the whole experience was a little surreal, but it was all great fun.

Michelle was a big help to me too, explaining a little about each of the stations and their likely audience. She was very impressed, for instance, that I was going to be on Radio National, the equivalent of the UK's austere, news- and cricket-based Radio 4. Fran Kelly was the name of the presenter, so the producer had told me.

'Fran Kelly?' exclaimed Michelle. 'She's one of the country's most serious political journalists. She's more used to interviewing prime ministers!' And so it was one morning that she spent fifteen minutes on live national radio talking to me. About mullets.

ABC Perth was another amusing interview, despite the fact it took us several attempts to get a decent phone line, perhaps a symptom of the vastness of Australia. The presenter, Ian, talked at length with me about mullets, demonstrating a serious enthusiasm for the haircut himself.

'So what common characteristics do mullets have?' He asked me. 'What drives them?

I thought for a second.

'A very good question, Ian. I think . . . I think it's self-confidence, mixed with a bit of reclusiveness,' I said, suddenly putting on my best sociologist voice. 'They're getting rarer, so mullets are becoming harder to spot, but they remain just as proud of what they are.' I had no idea what I was saying, but it sounded good.

'You know Billy Ray Cyrus?'

'Yeah, rings a bell,' I replied. He was the famously mulleted singer of Achy Breaky Heart, Ian explained.

'And he's the mullet from HELL!' Ian boomed in his deep radio voice, the intensity of his declaration making me quite glad I was on the opposite side of the continent from him.

At the end of our chat, he thanked me for coming on, and reminded his listeners who he'd been speaking to: 'Simon Varwell' – he paused for a beat – 'mullet hunter.'

Simon Varwell: Mullet Hunter. I liked that.

Meanwhile, my television appearance was a quick five minutes by video-link from a studio near Brisbane to the Australian capital Canberra, where the presenter, just a talking head on a monitor to me, quizzed me about the mission for a regional show in rural Queensland that was part of a nation-wide commercial network, Southern Cross Ten. It was strange being on television, especially by video-link, but as I told myself it was just radio with pictures, and my by now near-perfect patter – practically free of *umms*, *ahs* and *you knows* – did just the job to raise a few laughs from the presenter.

Perhaps the most enjoyable interview I had, though, was with Rod Chester from the Brisbane Courier-Mail, whom I had emailed before coming to Australia and who was finally roused into action. This being for print, we were able to have a lengthier and more relaxed chat about my mission, unlike many of my radio interviews where I was conscious of being live and unable to swear or correct mistakes. Rod began by apologising for not being in touch with me sooner, but he had been busy with the commemorations of the end of World War Two. I didn't point out to him that he'd had sixty years to work on that particular story.

He asked me all about the beginnings of the mission, and I explained about how travelling with Niall had got me into mullets. He asked what Niall now thought of the mission.

'To be honest,' I replied, 'I think he's a bit perturbed. He was always the one into mullets, and now I've kind of taken it further than he'd ever have imagined. Perhaps I'm a bit like Anakin Skywalker, the rebellious apprentice. Er . . . without the desire to take over the galaxy,' I added hastily.

'Talking of galaxies, have you read the Hitch-Hiker's Guide to the Galaxy?' asked Rod.

'Yeah, years ago. I can't remember all of it though.'

'There was this one guy,' he reminded me, 'who took it upon himself to insult everyone in the whole universe. Only he gave up when he realised that people kept getting born and he'd never get to finish.'

'That sounds exactly like me with the mullets – whenever I visit one, I end up discovering more.' I replied. 'I came out here knowing of two, and found five.' I didn't mention the fifty that ABC Bundaberg had almost found me. 'I like to compare it to killing the Hydra from Greek mythology – you chop off one head, and two more appear. But I prefer your hitch-hiker's metaphor much more!'

'Are you married, Simon?' Rod asked.

'No, I replied.

'Then you need to find yourself a nice simple girl who works in a fish factory and doesn't mind you disappearing round the world for long periods of time to go hunt mullets.'

'I dunno, I am sure I can do a lot better than that.' I thought for a second. 'Though I am sure there are some perfectly pleasant people who work in fish factories.'

SIXTEEN

The Award of the Golden Mullet

In that last couple of days of my time in Australia, enjoying the last of Noel, Di and Michelle's kind and patient hospitality in amongst the media madness, there was a healthy stream of emails not just from journalists but from ordinary, lovely Australians who'd read or heard about the mission and just wanted to ask about it and wish me well.

Some people wrote to tell me about how they'd heard of the mission in their local paper or had heard me talk on the radio, while others told me about themselves and their experience of mullets. One guy for instance told me there was a mullet fish festival in a place called Bribie Island, should I be around any October in the future; while others reported sightings of awful mullet haircuts.

A man called Raymand did a bit of homework for me and found me a couple of other mullet placenames. He pointed me to Mullet Lake Park in Florida, and to a place in Mexico – called Tamanikawa – which was a native Mexican language translation for 'mullet place'. I liked that. It was in a Mexican tongue, but still had the word 'mullet' in its name. Just not in English. Perhaps it counted.

Then a girl in Montreal, Quebec, somehow heard about the story and got in touch in a similar vein. She told me that in French-speaking Canada, a mullet was called 'un coupe Long-ueuil'. She explained that Longueuil was a suburb of Montreal, the capital of Quebec, which was renowned for the mullet haircut. Again, I thought, the name didn't strictly contain the word 'mullet' but in another language it very much embodied it.

I even had the most amazing email from a lass in the south Australian city of Adelaide. I'll let you read it for yourselves:

Hi Simon.

I'm not sure if you're still in Australia, but a friend of mine read an article about you in our local newspaper which explained that you're travelling the world in search of destinations with the word 'mullet' in the title.

I thought I would let you know that here in Adelaide, South Australia, there is a touch football team known as the Mullets. We named our team after the mullet hairdo. Although this doesn't really fit your criteria since our footy team is not actually a place, I thought you might be interested anyway.

Touch football is like rugby, but less rough. We have a team of 14 players – 8 girls and 6 guys. None of us actually have a mullet cut, but some of us did back in the 1980s (as was the trend back then). We have our own newsletter called The Mullet Monthly, and it often features a column on Mullet Spotting. It's surprising how many mullets there are in Adelaide!

Anyway, if you are still in Australia, and anywhere near Adelaide, let me know and maybe you can come and watch a game and have a beer with us afterwards at the pub (which we often do as we're mainly a social team).

If you want to know anymore about our team, feel free to ask.

Cheers.

Natalie

We exchanged a couple of emails, and a couple of weeks later Natalie wrote back to explain something of the history behind the club.

Hi Simon.

Thanks for writing back.

I'm not sure exactly why we named the touch footy team 'The Mullets' . . . my friend and I were trying to think of a funny and different name for the team and originally came up with the Secret Mullet Society. This induced much laughter throughout the touch footy association (who didn't really take us very seriously) so we decided a few seasons later to shorten the name to The Mullets.

Since then, we have developed a tradition in the team of awarding the best and fairest players with the ultimate trophy – a Golden Mullet. At the end of every season we have The Golden Mullet Award Ceremony and Dinner. The winners are crowned with a special golden mullet wig (bought for two dollars from the local supermarket) and receive a bottle of wine.

I have attached a copy of our latest newsletters. It features a story on you (I think I referred to you as a bizarre Scotsman . . . no offence of course!!). It's mainly about the footy team and our winter season performance so far.

Also, below is the article about you that appeared in our local paper, The Advertiser.

Anyway, good to hear from you and if you ever visit Adelaide, you are very welcome to come and watch a game!

Regards
Natalie.

The Golden Mullet Award Ceremony!? And people called me mad . . .

Natalie's email proved two things to me. Firstly, that there were other people more obsessed with mullets than I, which I found reassuring. Secondly, that there were newspapers out there printing my story that I had not spoken to. A cursory search for articles on the web showed that many of them had much the same text. This made me realise just how lazy and unoriginal the press can be sometimes, just stealing articles off each other – much in the way that the Sydney Morning Herald had from the Bundie News-Mail. It was understandable, given the short deadlines and tight turnarounds that journalists would usually work to. If there's a quirky story ready-made that can fill a few inches, why waste too much time editing it?

I found it more fun engaging with random people around the world than with journalists around Australia, though. The media interviews were fun, don't get me wrong. It was definitely a novelty to know I was being heard by audiences of thousands while debating the relative merits of the skullet, or describing dried up creeks in rural Queensland. And it has been wonderful to this day to reflect on the fact that I've been in more Australian newspapers than I am entirely sure I know about.

However, it was great to hear from genuine people, who were probably just like me, leading ordinary lives, doing ordinary jobs and living in ordinary places, who were inspired, encouraged and entertained by what I was doing.

Recently I had been struggling to identify why exactly I was still pursuing the mission.

When I first conceived the quest that bored afternoon at work in Inverness, I wanted to do it just because I could. Then I carried on because it was exciting, and involved travelling to new and interesting places. Though I'd had a great time down under, it hadn't always been exciting. My Australian tour had on occasions been a little bit lonely, frustrating and (when ABC Bundaberg dropped their bombshell) positively depressing.

In writing to me out of the blue, however, people reminded me that the mission served another purpose – to raise a few smiles, to catch people's imagination, and to inspire them that if they also strongly wanted to do something but worried that it was a little bit silly, they just had to get on with it and do it, and enjoy it as much as possible.

One woman called Elizabeth Stevenson wrote me a very short, very simple and very friendly email:

Just saying 'hello' from Mudgee in New South Wales, Australia! I was amused by your search for the Mullet places of the world.

Good luck on your journey and stay crazy. The world needs people like you.

Her email had a profound effect on me as I read it.

On the one hand, the media interest had proved to me that if and when I tackled the rest of the mullets, now clustered mostly across the Americas, from Canada to the Falkland Islands, I could succeed. I was confident that I had the ability to generate interest before my arrival that would help me track down locations, and unearth local information and local assistance, meaning I could really make the most of each trip.

In short, it had given me renewed confidence for completing the mission.

But Elizabeth's email had done something else, something more. While the media had shown me that I *could* do it, she'd shown me that I *must* do it.

The world needed crazy people like me.